# BIBLICAL LAW OF ATTRACTION FOR DIFFICULT SPOUSES

By

## Jeremy Lopez

Biblical Law of Attraction for Difficult
Spouses
By Dr. Jeremy Lopez
Copyright © 2018

Published by Identity Network
P.O. box 383213
Birmingham, AL 35238

www.IdentityNetwork.net

# ENDORSEMENT

*"You are put on this earth with incredible potential and a divine destiny. This powerful, practical man shows you how to tap into powers you didn't even know you had."* – Brian Tracy – Author, The Power of Self Confidence

*"I found myself savoring the concepts of the Law of Attraction merging with the Law of Creativity until slowly the beautiful truths seeped deeper into my thirsty soul. I am called to be a Creator! My friend, Dr. Jeremy Lopez, has a way of reminding us of our eternal 'I-Am-ness' while putting the tools in our hands to unlock our endless creative potential with the Divine mind. As a musical composer, I'm excited to explore, with greater understanding, the infinite realm of possibilities as I place fingers on my piano and whisper, 'Let there be!'"* – Dony McGuire, Grammy Award winning artist and musical composer

*"Jeremy dives deep into the power of consciousness and shows us that we can create a world where the champion within us can shine and how we can manifest our desires to live a life of fulfillment. A must read!"* – Greg S. Reid – Forbes and Inc. top rated Keynote Speaker

*"I have been privileged to know Jeremy Lopez for many years, as well as sharing the platform with him at a number of conferences. Through this time, I have found him as a man of integrity, commitment, wisdom, and one of the most networked people I have met. Jeremy is an entrepreneur and a leader of leaders. He has amazing insights into leadership competencies and values. He has a passion to ignite this latent potential within individuals and organizations and provide ongoing development and coaching to bring about competitive advantage and success. I would recommend him as a speaker, coach, mentor, and consultant."* – Chris Gaborit – Learning Leader, Training & Outsourcing Expert, Entrepreneur

# CONTENTS

# PREFACE

The scriptures declare that love is the greatest of all spiritual gifts – far greater than even prophecy. As we think of life and of the many, many moments of time which pass as we live our lives, we find ourselves reminded that in each passing moment, it is the people in our lives who matter most. With all of our successes and all of our triumphs we experience, they truly mean very little without the joy that accompanies sharing such moments with the people we love. Life is filled with many remarkable and wonderful spiritual connections and relationships and learning to view all of our relationships the way GOD sees them is essential to prospering in all areas of life. Of all the many relationships we encounter throughout life, though, there is one connection which stands out and towers above all the rest. Of all relationships, we enjoy, there is a union which is blessed and honored, perhaps, more than all others – the marriage relationship. So often, when providing prophetic counseling and coaching to various clients throughout the world, the questions I seem to be asked most are the questions concerning love and relationships. More than questions concerning business success, more than questions concerning the awakening of prophetic gifts, and even more than questions concerning ways to build lasting success in ministry, I find myself constantly being asked about love and marriage.

Yet, in truth, how does one even begin to define the concept of love? Truly, it is such a powerful and heavenly gift that our words seem to do very little justice. Actually, if you think about it, to even be assigned the task of defining "love" would be akin to being asked to define the term "GOD." Such a task seems almost impossible to the natural mind. However, according to the scriptures, the two are one in the same. GOD *is* love. Love *is* GOD. Just as we often find ourselves grappling to understand GOD, though, as we go throughout life, we often times also find ourselves questioning even the existence of love. In loving, passionate relationships – particularly in marriage – there can be some pretty difficult moments. There are times in which confusion arises and fears and uncertainty begin to abound. For each question regarding love and relationships, I am asked, equally as much, "Jeremy, why is my spouse so difficult?" *That*, my friend, is the reason for this book. I recently released a best-selling book series called *Attracting Your Godly Spouse*. The response to the release of the book and the subsequent workbook and accompanying study guide has been phenomenal. Literally thousands of testimonies have poured into the offices of Identity Network as men and women, both old and young, expressed how radically their lives have been transformed as they've begun to recognize the voice of the Holy Spirit in all of their relationships. Other testimonies have expressed how, after beginning to implement the techniques and principles shared within the book, new dating relationships have begun, engagements have been celebrated, and marriages have been forged. It's amazing, really, the miracles that happen when we begin to include GOD in our love lives.

However, for those who are married, there is even more to be said. Truthfully, *that* is the reason for this book. In marriage, there are times of testing, times of heartbreak, and times of confusion and uncertainty. Let's face it. In marriage, there are times when things – when the other person – can seem so very difficult to deal with. Today, if you find yourself in a marriage relationship and overcome with the seemingly constant stress and with what seems to be a never ending battle with your own special someone, this book is for you. As I shared in my latest book, not only is love worth finding, but love is worth keeping. My prayer for you, today, is that as you read the pages of this book, you will once again be reminded of the beauty of your own love story. Truly, love conquers all. However, realizing that powerful truth is just the beginning. Saying "I do" is not enough. To keep the love you've found requires saying, "I *still* do.

# INTRODUCTION

Love is patient and love is kind, but sometimes we are not. Love endures all things and always hopes for the best. Sometimes, though, we, as human beings would much rather take the easy way out and choose, instead, to see only the worst. We all have so much to learn, and I, for one, am so very thankful for the leading of the Holy Spirit and the grace of GOD. We know that love is patient and that love is kind. We know this truth so much, in fact, that we can often take the power of love for granted. When writing my best-selling book *Attracting Your Godly Spouse*, I felt led by the Holy Spirit to include a chapter that detailed the importance of "keeping" the love we find, even when things seem so very difficult. Far, far too often, when the going gets tough, the not-so-tough simply walk away. When we finally do attract into our lives the love and passion-filled romance we desire and when that love leads to marriage, well, then what? What comes next? What happens when the honeymoon period ends and cold, hard reality begins to set in? What happens when love becomes difficult? Well, that's the reason for this book. For every person who contacts me to inquire of the LORD when they will find their own Godly spouse, I receive four times as many questions from heartbroken and anxious, beautiful individuals who ask, "Jeremy, why does my marriage seem so difficult?" I share this with you to point out, quite simply, although love *is* patient; love will often try *our* patience. So, what is the answer, really? Are we all simply destined for continued moments of heartbreak, stress, and anxiety, fated to simply have to continue living lives of constant struggle where love is concerned? Absolutely not! There is a better way.

As with all things worth holding onto, though, recognizing the answer will require a much-needed shift in perspective. If you're reading this book, chances are you now find yourself battling with a difficult spouse or love interest. Chances are, in fact, you're now finding yourself asking, "Is it even worth it?" If you were to be completely honest with yourself, chances are you'd admit that on more than one occasion you've questioned whether or not to simply throw in the towel and walk away. Although there, in fact, are very real reasons to walk away, I thank GOD that you've been led to this book. As we begin this journey together, I want to make you a promise. Although it isn't easy right now and although it might feel like making the decision to walk down the aisle was one of the worst decisions of your life, if you will enter into this book and these teachings and techniques with an open mind, a prayer-filled heart, and an even greater sensitivity to the voice of the Holy Spirit, you will gain a newfound sense of clarity and will, at the very least, begin to see your significant other in a much more heavenly and loving way. Often, all we need is a simple shift of perspective and a reminder of what actually began the love in the first place.

Right now, as you begin this book, I want you to visualize within your mind the moment that you first met your own special someone. See it, and allow yourself to really *feel* that moment. The overwhelming love and desire was intoxicating, wasn't it? In an instant, it seemed, you found yourself able to view the rest of your life with that person. Everything felt very magical in that moment. Along with the sense of desire came an otherworldly, heavenly chemistry so intense it sometimes kept you up at night. Days were filled with conversations which lasted for hours at a time. However, somewhere along the way, something began to change, didn't it? Maybe careers got in the way. Then the children came along. The bills continued to mount. Love, it seemed, was replaced with a sense of stress and unfamiliarity. The assurance you once had was replaced by a feeling of the unknown. Before you knew it, months and even years had passed. Now, maybe it seems like your significant other is unrecognizable to you. Somewhere along the way, "I love you" became lost in translation. Somewhere along the way, "I want you" devolved into "I don't want *this*." It's alright to admit that.

Healing and freedom always begin in truth. Truth, though, can often times be very uncomfortable and highly, highly inconvenient. By being able to admit your own unhappiness and your own sense of dissatisfaction, you are beginning to come into your own, greater honesty. As we begin this journey together, I want to commend you, here at the offset, for even wanting to take the time to try to "fix" it. Perhaps, as you now read these words, you look back over the months and years when you invested so much and you now find yourself, saying, "Jeremy, I have nothing left to give." Well, the very fact that you're now reading these words signals to me and to all of Heaven that there is still hope. I want you to know that, before we go any further. There is always hope, and hope maketh not ashamed. Though you may not realize it now, you possess much more power than you're giving yourself credit for. It's true, as much as it may not seem like it right now. You are the co-creator of your life and the co-creator of your own, unique love story. If you now find yourself unhappy and dissatisfied with the love story you now live, thankfully, it's possible to recreate and to begin again. You see, that's the amazing, beautiful power of the Biblical Law of Attraction within our lives. You and I are always, always, always given the opportunity to recreate and to begin anew. Beginning to recreate, though, requires being able to reassess and to recalibrate. New beginnings always require a shift in perspective. Change demands accepting personal responsibility. The Kingdom of Heaven demands that we confront often painful truths if we are ever going to progress and to move into greater glories.

Love brings with it its own growing pains and birthing pains. These pains are rarely ever welcomed and more times than not seem like such devastation. But what if I were to tell you that these growing pains – these very messy and difficult moments – were actually designed by GOD to cause you to surrender even more deeply to the love you have? What if I told you that, in spite of the stress and the anger that now seems to arise in your marriage on a daily basis, GOD is wanting to change you? I know, I know, you're thinking, "But Jeremy, the issue isn't me; the issue is my difficult spouse." I understand. But did you know that the same creative, attractive, heavenly power of GOD which you used to first attract into your life the love and relationship you had so longed for is the exact same power that will be required to maintain and to keep that relationship working? Throughout my book, *Attracting Your Godly Spouse*, I continually referenced the vast and limitless power of the Biblical Law of Attraction. This creative power was first established at the very beginning of Creation when GOD decreed "Let there be." The same power of creative, heavenly force is still very much alive, active, and even now residing within your very own thoughts. It's time to change your mind about your marriage and about yourself. Stop giving credit to the enemy and begin to, once again, harness the power of the Godhead within you.

Some fifteen years ago, a young woman reached out to me to inquire of the Holy Spirit. After suffering a series of heartbreaks and relationships that seemed to end long before they ever really began, she asked, "Jeremy, when will I find the love of my life?" Under the unction of the Holy Ghost, I shared with her the powerful principles I outlined within *Attracting Your Godly Spouse*. To my great joy, within only a matter of five months, she reported back the testimony that she had recently become engaged to, as she put it, her "dream come true."

I was overjoyed for her and joined her in giving GOD thanks, and I also congratulated her on the accomplishment of fully utilizing her own creative, attractive power to manifest the love of her life. Time went by. Five years to be exact. When she reached out again, it seemed everything had changed. "Jeremy, I can't take another day of this torment," she expressed. I felt the genuine and sincere pain in her soul as she spoke to me. Her pain was not merely a feeling of discomfort but of heartbreak. "He's not the man I married," she said, choking back tears. "We just can't seem to agree on, well, anything these days." She went on to share how two years after their vows they welcomed the birth of their first daughter. Then, the following year, the son came along. "Jeremy, everything changed. It's like we don't even know each other anymore." My heart broke for her beautiful family, as I listened intently to her story. She explained, "We've tried marriage counseling. We've been counseled by our pastor. We've received words from the LORD from other prophets. Nothing seems to be working." I felt the tangible sense of desperation. "We haven't even been intimate in more than nine months." To the natural eye, admittedly, it seemed that there was nothing left to do but end the marriage. But then I heard it. Within my spirit, I heard the Word of the LORD as clearly as ever before say, "This isn't over yet. There's still hope."

My friend, even as I write these words to you, once again I feel that same anointing and that same unction to declare to you concerning your marriage, "This isn't over yet! There's *still* hope!" Today, as we embark upon this journey into what I firmly believe will become the greatest chapter of your marriage and into a true and lasting intimacy and closeness that can only come from the creative, attractive power of the Holy Spirit, I want to encourage you to try once more. You might just be surprised to find that the answers you were seeking were *within* your very own self all along. Now, please understand, I'm in no way suggesting that you should live another day in fear or in torment, and in no way am I seeking to suggest that you don't have the right to find your very own happiness. What I am saying, though, is that until you've tried the secrets of the Biblical Law of Attraction concerning your marriage, there's still hope. So, with that, I make you this promise, my beautiful friend. If you will begin to harness your own creative, attractive power once again – the same power which brought into your life the love you once craved – you will experience the power of resurrection in your marriage. It isn't over *yet*, and believe me when I say that the entirety of Heaven and all of earth can be moved on your behalf in just an instant. If you will commit to being open to the voice of the Holy Spirit and to the leading of the LORD and if you will commit to putting into practice the principles and techniques I share within this book, change will begin to manifest in the most miraculous and magical of ways. *That* I assure you. My friend, in spite of the pain and in spite of the difficulty, it's time to dream again.

# CHANGE COMES

*"We all change.   We all grow.   We all evolve.   We all move from glory to glory."* – *Jeremy Lopez*

It can be the most frightening and most horrifying thing in existence, really.  It shakes us to our very core and causes us to not only question our own lives and our own beliefs but also, at times, our very own faith.  I'm talking about "change."  When change comes, so, too, does the uncertainty and the fear of the unknown.  Change, as frightening as it can be, often takes on an even more terrifying form when it comes to our marriage.  As we see the person we've committed to begin to change, seemingly before our eyes, not only are walls of guardedness raised and lines of separation drawn, but, also, the fear can become overwhelming. As we see the person to whom we've committed ourselves begin to change and to evolve into someone completely different, we begin to instinctively wrestle with our own, inner insecurities. "What does this mean?" "What will the future hold?" "Can we survive?" Although change is a very inconvenient element of life within the Kingdom, there can be no denying the simple fact that in life and in our marriage relationships, changes will come.

There is no denying it and no escaping it. When one or both spouses begin to change, suddenly, seemingly out of nowhere, the foundation of the marriage is questioned, as one or both partners begin to ask, "Is this what we truly wanted?" It can be easy to question our visions for the future whenever changes come. This happens, in part, because at the very core of our being we are driven to have a need for control and, in part, because insecurity, itself, is fueled by the element of the unknown. Allow me to explain. Change causes us to consider the durability and sustainability of our foundation by allowing us to be shaken to our very core. When change comes, so, too, does fear, often times. But did you know that it doesn't have to be this way? Did you know that change, though frightening, doesn't have to be as debilitating as we would like to believe? I want to say, first of all, that it's time to begin to view the element of change in a much more heavenly and spiritual way. Sure, chances are your spouse isn't the exact same person he or she was when you met, but the brutal truth of the matter is that neither are you. By the divine design of a loving and caring Creator, we all grow, we all change, and we all evolve. The scriptures make it plain that we are continuously being inspired to move and to grow into greater glories. *"But we all, with open face beholding as in a glass the glory of the Lord, are changed into the same image from glory to glory, even as by the Spirit of the Lord." (2 Corinthians 3:18 KJV)* Notice that the passage specifically makes mention of change coming to "all." Not one of us is exempt from change.

For far, far too long you've based your security upon your own sense of familiarity and, as a result, you haven't recognized the changes that accompany growth. My friend, you're growing and evolving and so, too, is your spouse. Not only is growth a very real principle of the Kingdom of Heaven, but growth is also a much needed catalyst for the Biblical Law of Kingdom Attraction. You see, by the divine design of GOD, you and I are created to be visual beings – powerful, seeing spirits capable of casting vision. However, often, when we see change begin to occur and when what we see before our natural eyes doesn't seem to align with our own vision of stability, we become shaken. This is why it is vitally important to be led by the voice of the Holy Spirit and to see all change through the eyes of GOD, rather than from the perspective of natural, temporal feelings. This is also another reason why it is so, so very important to recognize that as you are being changed and as you are continuing to grow, so is your spouse, and you have to allow them that freedom. So often, when coaching couples in marriage relationships, I hear, "He just isn't the same person he was when we met." Usually, within my spirit I often think, "Well, that's a great thing!" You see, my friend, as growth begins to occur, change happens and, though frightening at times to the ego and the desire to control, these changes are necessary to propel us into greater glories. You are not the person you were five years ago. In fact, the truth is that you aren't really the same person that you were last week or even yesterday. With the passing of time comes new revelation and new experience. Our desires change. Our tastes change. Interests change. Can you imagine a world in which we were all identical? What a very drab and boring existence it would be. When the Creator fashioned man from the dust of the earth and breathed into him the very breath of life and when He, thereafter, drew from his side "woman," it was revealed to the new world for the very first time the amazing and heavenly beauty of difference.

Differences have existed from the very beginning, in the garden paradise – not as a way to create conflict but, rather, as a way for the Creator to express his own all-powerful creativity. So often, rather than honoring the unique differences we have, we would prefer to control and to cause others to conform to our own interpretations. This can be especially true in marriage relationships, as one or both partners begin to stifle the growth of the other. As you look back over the course of your life, can you honestly say that you're the same person you once were? Of course not. With the passing of time and with greater knowledge have come lessons learned, new revelation, a greater sense of self-discovery, and, above all, newfound identity. As difficult as it is for the ego to accept, it is truly a great hypocrisy, really, to allow your own self room to grow and to change while refusing to give others within your life that same exact freedom. I can still vividly remember coaching a married couple once who had reached out to the offices of Identity Network for relationship counseling. Their names were Ashley and Brian. Ashley, a successful account executive, expressed to me how after only two years of marriage, Brian had begun to seem so distant and so disconnected. "It's like he's someone else," she said. "He says he wants something new." Ashley and Brian had met while she was in college, completing her master's degree. Brian had, for years, worked for his father's moving company. For Brian, he had always felt a sense of obligation to carry on the family business; however, he was unsatisfied. As Ashley completed her degree, Brian supported her completely in her endeavors.

Then, one day, some two years into the marriage, Brian decided to embark upon a new career path for himself. Brian, being ever the dreamer, had decided that he wanted to go into business for himself and launch a career in writing. It was so completely different. In only a matter of weeks, it seemed that everything had begun to change. Brian began writing and within only a matter of weeks completed his very first manuscript to shop to publishers. "He's not the same Brian," Ashley said in desperation and through tears. Immediately, as she spoke, I sensed the Holy Spirit reveal to me the true root of the issue. "Ashley is failing to honor Brian's growth." You see, my friend, as growth begins to occur, so often we choose to see only the change. When witnessing the divine element of growth and choosing to see only the changes that are occurring, we can so often become judgmental, critical, and, therefore, stifled in our own growth. Although Brian had supported Ashley's dream and career path from the very beginning, when Brian felt the leading of the Holy Spirit to begin to dream a new dream for himself, Ashley found herself refusing to allow him room for his own growth. Rather than seeing growth and opportunity and expansion, Ashley could see only the drastic changes. As she spoke, I immediately, by the Spirit, sensed the underlying fear within her words. At the root of the issue, Ashley was fearful that Brian would become successful and no longer find satisfaction and joy within the marriage. This, however, was not the case. Brian loved Ashely with his entire being and wanted only room to grow into his own dream and Holy Spirit-inspired destiny. Today, now the proud parents of three children, Ashley and Brian are now thriving in their marriage and Brian is a successful author of five children's books. With Brian's growth came, also, increased financial security. When Ashley began to allow her spouse the freedom to grow, in spite of the fear that accompanied the apparent "changes," she found herself in an even greater sense of intimacy and closeness with her spouse.

As I write these words, I'm reminded of the ever-popular song by the band Journey, entitled "Faithfully." The song, written to paint the picture of a love affair rekindled after time away, paints beautifully the importance of learning. In the song, Steve Perry sings, "I get the joy of rediscovering you." You see, in marriage, it truly isn't enough to discover your partner. You must continually re-discover them, over and over again. This is because change comes and with change so, too, does growth. Rather than criticizing the changes you see in your spouse, why not begin to ask, "How am I contributing to the growth the Holy Spirit is inspiring within them?" You might just be pleasantly surprised to see the newfound level of intimacy and understanding that will begin to arise the moment you stop criticizing and warring against change and begin to, instead, see change as a needed element of growth into even greater glories. My friend, GOD wants your marriage to thrive; however, that cannot happen without growth, and growth looks a lot like "change." Rather than being fearful, start to become even more faithful. Faithful in your own sensitivity to the Holy Spirit. Faithful to honor and to recognize the unique gifts within your partner. And, above all, faithful to embrace the unexpected changes that always accompany growth into new dimensions.

# A HEAVENLY PARTNERSHIP

When GOD instituted marriage in the very beginning of it all, He set a heavenly mandate for partnership. Marriage is a heavenly union, and in order to begin to tackle the difficult task of dealing with a difficult spouse, you're going to have to, first, recognize that partnerships require the willing participation of both participants. You've, I'm sure, heard the old, familiar adage "It takes two to tango." As cliché as it might seem, the old saying is absolutely true – particularly in the divine and heavenly union of marriage. For generations, you and I have been taught the importance of being "equally yoked." Often, though, the truth of partnership has been taught to us by the church in a rather extreme and often-times unbiblical way. Perhaps you know, firsthand, what I mean by this. When we were first taught the importance of being equally yoked together, we were told, quite simply, that we should have no fellowship with those of different beliefs. More specifically even, we were taught that a believer should never, under any circumstances whatsoever, enter the covenant of marriage with an unbeliever. The results, we were taught, are always, always catastrophic.

However, given that the divorce rate is the same within the church as it is within the world, I would argue that the idea of being "equally yoked" means something much different than what you and I were once led to believe. Since many divorces occur between two sincere believers of the Christian faith, obviously the referenced passage of scripture means much more than we might have once cared to consider. In other words, it's time to move from the place of legalistic religion and into the greater dimensions of the truth of the Holy Spirit. In case you haven't noticed it yet, religion rarely, if ever, seems to be able to provide the answer. Only the Holy Spirit can do that, and it is only the Holy Spirit who is capable of leading into all truth. Am I seeking to suggest in any way that partnerships between fellow believers are unbeneficial? Absolutely not. However, what I am saying, though, is that it's time we begin to view the idea of partnership in a much more mature and adult way, from the perspective of personal responsibility rather than religious dogma. For years, in countless coaching sessions with married couples, I've often seen the dangers that can arise when we place upon our spouse or significant other our own preprogrammed ideas of truth. Often times, what we call "truth" is simply our own egos seeking to control and to manipulate our partners, in an attempt to convince them to become more like us.

Yes, truth does exist, thankfully. However, so, too, does the journey of life, and in order to begin to come to the place of mutual understanding and a shared common goal, responsibility is required on the parts of both spouses within the marriage – most notably the responsibility of becoming more understanding. *"Be ye not unequally yoked together with unbelievers: for what fellowship hath righteousness with unrighteousness? and what communion hath light with darkness?" (2 Corinthians 6:14 KJV)* In the referenced scripture, the Apostle Paul admonishes the early church at Corinth to be ever-vigilant to guard and to protect their faith; however, the "darkness" he references isn't some malevolent force of evil as much as it is a reference to spiritual awakening and spiritual understanding.

All throughout the entirety of the holy scriptures, the imagery of darkness is used as an analogy to depict a lack of understanding and a state of confusion or ignorance. How often have we allowed a sense of apparent "darkness" into our relationships simply because we failed to even try to be understanding of our spouses? How often has a feeling of "darkness" crept into the union of marriage, quite simply, because one or both partners simply chose to fuel a sense of disrespect or judgment rather than a sense of honor and acknowledgement? This is all too common even in Christian marriages, so obviously the Apostle Paul is speaking of a greater, more transcendent truth than whether or not a couple can agree on which church to attend. Again, it's time to move beyond religion and into the far greater truth of the Kingdom of Heaven.

A successful marriage is a lesson in understanding and a lesson in partnership. When a client comes to me for marriage coaching, determined to list all of the negative and unseemly qualities of his or her spouse, I ask, "Well, does he provide for you?" "Does she listen and is she caring and nurturing?" "Is he a good father?" "Is she a good mother?" "Does he make time for you?" "Does he go out of his way to make time for you?" So often, the answers to these questions are "Yes." I then say, "Well, if the only issue you have is that he doesn't want to go to church with you, it seems like you have a better marriage than some." You see, my friend, far too often we place upon our partners our own religious programming and our own desire to control, forgetting, at times, that it is the Holy Spirit who leads into all truth. Your role within your marriage partnership is to be understanding and encouraging and to honor the changes that accompany growth as the marriage progresses. The issue I so often find, though, is that in most marriages, rather than there being a bond of genuine partnership, there is simply a dictatorship. Many times, when I hear in coaching sessions, "He isn't the same person," what I'm actually interpreting is, "He isn't who I expect him to be." You see, partnership, by definition, requires the honoring of the association – a constant recognition of the mutual bond.

Not only does this require a great sense of understanding but it also requires an enormous amount of mutually shared respect. When disagreements arise and when seemingly difficult moments ensue in marriages, most couples often lose all sense of the respect they once shared when first entering into the marriage. When respect is gone, rather than a desire to seek understanding, there comes the desire to be right, to prove points, and to say the most cutting, hurtful, and unnecessary of words. Words that can never be taken back. I often think that if we can simply become more conscientious of the power behind our own words, we would see such a decrease and such a de-escalation of most of our arguments and unnecessary heated exchanges. When the sense of respect begins to become lost or neglected – or simply thrown away – a self-fulfilling prophecy begins to become enacted. Things begin to quickly spiral out of control and become far less manageable. The energy of creation only heightens the feeling of emotional turmoil and disarray, as our thoughts of anger and resentment continue to fuel the chaos we create.

If you can enter into your moments with, at the bare minimum, a sense of respect for your partner, then you will begin to see a tremendous difference in the outcome of even the most difficult of moments, I assure you. There is much to be said about the importance of respect. The dictionary defines the term *respect* as "a feeling of deep admiration for someone or something elicited by their abilities, qualities, or achievements." Although, in heated moments, it can understandably be very difficult to lose sight of the positive, as emotions become heightened and anger arises, if you can take but a second to remember that your spouse possesses amazing qualities which attracted you to them in the beginning, I promise you will find it much, much more difficult to say such hurtful, cutting things and make such unnecessary remarks. In fact, you may even begin to recognize and be reminded that the partnership is actually much stronger and more heavenly than you've ever taken the time to truly notice. Respect is essential in all of our many relationships in life; however, where the heavenly and divine union of marriage is concerned, respect is foundational.

Even though your "difficult" spouse, in the moment, may be exhibiting the most unattractive and seemingly horrible qualities, rather than allowing your response to be based upon the heated, triggered emotions, begin to respond in a more conscientious way – from the level of respect. There's a reason you married your partner. There's a reason you decided to exchange vows. There's a reason the chemistry existed at one time – even if it may now seem so nonexistent. There's a reason that you decided to commit yourself and the remainder of your life to your spouse. I would respectfully urge you, my friend, to not lose sight of the many amazing qualities your partner does possess simply because, in certain moments, difficulties arise. Partnerships of all types require a remembrance of the common goal. As a success coach and prophetic counselor, I often like to think of the term "partnership" from the perspective of business success. A partnership is an alliance between two or more people for the pursuit of a common goal or target. In all partnerships, there must be a shared vision – an intended target in mind. When difficulties arise and when the confusion that so often accompanies emotion begins to set in, I would urge you to at least remember your common, shared goal. In spite of the difficult moments, there is a common goal and there is an expected end in sight.

So often, in my coaching sessions with married couples, what I find is that the moment couples can be reminded of their commonalities and of the fact that it was a common shared feeling which inspired the attraction and chemistry in the very beginning, the "difficulties" begin to seem more and more insignificant and trivial, until, may times, they simply vanish away into nothingness. Your marriage is your vow before GOD of your intention to enter into partnership. In your own heavenly partnership, in spite of any difficulty or heightened emotion, always, always maintain a          sense          of          respect.

# THE ENERGY OF MARRIAGE

*"Everything is energy, even marriage."* - *Jeremy Lopez*

There's a reason I felt led by the Holy Spirit to entitle this book *Biblical Law of Attraction for Difficult Spouses*, as you might have already recognized. For more than twenty years, in prophetic ministry and life coaching, I've found that there exists, at the root of all of life's moments, a very powerful energy of creative force. Everything is energy – literally *everything*. Even your marriage. Allow me to explain. In the very beginning of it all, in the account of the story of Creation, we find that GOD spoke. Well, before GOD spoke, GOD, first, visualized and thought. The scriptures reveal to us that all of Creation was enacted by the powerful force of creation, the instant GOD spoke. In order for the Godhead, though, to manifest His desire and form and create the worlds within the universe, He, first needed a vision within His own mind. Before you and I were ever even formed within the wombs of our mothers, we existed within the heart and the mind of GOD. So, too, did your marriage, whether you realize it or not. In other words, everything began with a thought.

Years ago, when first beginning to recognize my own prophetic gifting, I began to become aware of just how powerful our own thoughts are. Our thoughts form the very basis of all of our life experiences. Although it may seem like quite a bitter pill to swallow and though it may seem to be quite an inconvenient truth to accept, literally every element of your life is now existing because of what you are thinking. From your career path to your finances to your emotions and, yes, even to your marriage, your own thoughts are creating the world you now find yourself living within. The life that you awakened to today is the direct result of yesterdays' thoughts. This powerful Biblical principle is evidenced even within your marriage to your difficult spouse. It was the Biblical Law of Attraction which began the attraction and sparked the chemistry in the beginning of your connection. It was this powerful, Biblical law which led to the marriage and the exchanging of vows. And, believe it or not, it is this same, powerful, universal law which is fueling even the difficult moments within your marriage. Again, it must be said that everything – literally *everything* – exists based entirely upon the Biblical Law of Attraction. Allow me to explain.

Long before the loving Creator reached down with His own hands into the dust of the newly formed earth to fashion the hallmark of His creation in His own image and likeness, He had within His mind and heart a vision of what the future would hold. In other words, He didn't just create carelessly or haphazardly. No. Rather, He gave great and careful thought to His Creation. There was an expected, intended result in mind all throughout the process of creation. Even after man was placed within the garden paradise, though, the power of creation continued to be enacted and was in full operation, because man, himself, had been infused with the very essence of the creative power of the Godhead. GOD had breathed into Him His very own breath. He then established that man would have dominion over all the earth, based entirely upon his own will and desires. Fast forward, now, to your own life, today. Today, although you are still a powerful, thinking, creative spirit, possessing all the power of the Godhead, the simple fact of the matter is that where your marriage is concerned, you've been creating carelessly and without much thought to detail.

Rather than focusing upon what you do want to create, you've been choosing, instead, to focus upon what you don't want. Well, the universe and all of Heaven and earth have taken notice of your thoughts, and because of this, you're getting even more of what you truly don't want! The truth, my friend, is that there isn't a prayer or a deliverance service that can change this, because GOD has already invested within you all the power necessary to create and to enact change. Right now, as you read these words, chances are you now find yourself living a life that you aren't enjoying, in a marriage that seems to be draining the literal life force out of you. My question to you, today, is what have you done to contribute to this? I know, at first thought, you want to blame your difficult spouse for all of the chaos that seems to be ensuing. We will deal with your spouse in a moment; however, the question is posed to you, personally. What are *you* doing to contribute to the environment of the chaos, based upon your thoughts?

For more than twenty years, after being led to greater prophetic awakening within my own life, I have come to realize, day by day and moment by moment, that we are not victims in this life. By divine, intelligent design, you and I have been infused to possess all the creative power of the Godhead. In the scriptures of the Holy Bible, two passages depict this powerful and transcendent truth perhaps more than all others. Proverbs 23:7 declares, *"For as he thinketh in his heart, so is he."* And Proverbs 29:18 says, *"Where there is no vision, the people perish: but he that keepeth the law, happy is he."* My dear friend, may I respectfully submit to you that the reason you're now living with such unhappiness, confusion, anger, resentment, and frustration in your marriage isn't really because of your difficult spouse but, rather, because you've forgotten or have neglected the creative, heavenly power of your own creative thoughts. It's time to begin to reclaim your own power once again. The same creative and attractive power which began your love story is the same exact creative power which is able to keep and to heal and to, above all, sustain your love story, and it's high time you begin to recognize that. Sure, it's easy to cast blame and to neglect responsibility. However, to neglect your own creative role is to simply doom your marriage for failure.

There is a better, much more heavenly way and that way is the Biblical Law of Attraction. It's time to begin to view your marriage and, more specifically, your difficult spouse in a much different and more heavenly way – through the eyes of a creator. I know that right now you probably think, "But Jeremy, you have no idea just how difficult my spouse can be." I understand. Again, we'll get to your difficult spouse in a moment, I promise. However, before we do, I want to encourage you, first, to begin to reclaim your own power and destiny as a divine, spiritual creator. Until you do that, nothing will ever change, I assure you. Is your spouse difficult, at times? Of course. Can the stresses and difficulties of the marriage be so overwhelming at times that they nearly drive you toward a breaking point? Absolutely. However, the power rests within you. You can either continue to react, or you can, through the power of the Holy Spirit, begin to act within your true role as a creator and begin to see the power of your own thoughts. You can either see yourself as a victim, or you can begin to take control. Taking control, though, will require doing the often painful work of looking within the mirror and taking personal responsibility. Until you do that, my friend, nothing will ever change.

I want to ask you a very simple question, and I want you to be completely honest with yourself. What are you truly thinking about your own marriage and about your own difficult spouse? It's time to go deeper in order to answer that question. The way in which you answer that question will determine whether or not you will continue to live a life of unhappiness or begin to live a life of abundance and contentment within your marriage. It's time to begin to do the work. Rather than casting blame, it's time to take ownership of your own thoughts again. You may say, "But Jeremy, he pushes me to by breaking point." Well, thankfully, you haven't broken yet, and GOD is giving you a chance, today, to begin to reclaim your own creative power of attraction. Today, I want to encourage you to begin to recognize that, even though it often doesn't seem like it and even though your spouse may very well be incredibly difficult to deal with, you and only you are responsible for your reactions. You are in control of yourself. Although it isn't our role or responsibility to change other people, we are responsible for mastering our own thought forms. And, miraculously enough, you will soon find that when you begin to take charge of your own thought life, your spouse will begin to change as well. Several years ago, I shared this powerful principle of thought with a young woman who had come to me for marriage coaching. She admitted to me, through tears, that she had been contemplating divorce because, as she explained, the marriage just wasn't "working." In her words, "He's just not making it work." She casually decided to omit the part about her cheating on her husband with her co-worker – which the Holy Spirit revealed to me. However, there is always hope and there is always, always grace, even in our most messy and chaotic and irresponsible of moments, thankfully. She simply said to me, "Jeremy, he's driven me to do the most horrible of things." I stopped her and reminded her that although GOD can, will, and does change the lives of people and although the Holy Spirit does, indeed, renew the minds of all men and women, GOD will never alleviate us of doing the work of taking personal responsibility for our own actions and our own thoughts. I lovingly reminded her of the importance of taking responsibility for her own thought life and reclaiming her own creative power. She was unconsciously creating much of the misery she was experiencing and, although her spouse was far from perfect, himself, she was contributing to the turmoil based upon her mindset.

Whether you realize it yet or not, you are the architect and the co-creator of your life based upon what you think about yourself. The issue, in truth, isn't really your difficult spouse. The issue, for you, is what you're choosing to think about your marriage and your difficult spouse. Although you aren't responsible for the actions or the behavior of your spouse, you are entirely, wholeheartedly responsible for your own actions and the way choose to react. Reaction isn't simply some flippant response that's the result of being triggered; it's a choice you make. In the midst of chaos and difficulty in your marriage, you are being given a choice to either contribute to the turmoil or to be an instrument of healing and clarity, based entirely upon what you choose to think and the thoughts you choose to give action to. It's time to become more thoughtful in your thoughts, more thoughtful in your responses, and much, much more cognizant of the thoughts you choose to dwell upon.

What you affirm, you will continue to manifest. There is no escaping the Biblical Law of Attraction. Rather than choosing to see only the bad and the negative, and affirming it, why not begin to see the good? Why not, instead, choose to focus upon the qualities and characteristics of your spouse that *are* admirable, attractive, and wonderful? Although you've probably stopped even trying to look for these amazing qualities because it seems that only the bad exists now, I assure you, your spouse, though "difficult" at times to deal with, possesses amazing qualities and still has a lot to offer. After all, isn't that the reason you felt the attraction and chemistry in the very beginning of the connection? One thing I've learned through years of prophetic coaching and training is that perspective is essential. In fact, it's our perspective which comprises literally 100% of all of our life experiences. Although in heated moments, it may seem difficult to recognize at first, the issue has never been your difficult spouse. The issue has always been the way that you are choosing to perceive your difficult spouse. By choosing to dwell upon the moments of conflict and the moments of disagreement, you are inadvertently choosing to affirm the bad and neglect the good. And as a result you are creating even more of what you claim to despise. This is the universal Law of Attraction at work. Allow me to give you an example to better explain this powerful, Biblical principle of creative attraction.

We are constantly attracting into our lives by our very thoughts. If I continue to confess, "I will not attract sickness," what I am inadvertently signaling to the universe and to all of Heaven is, in fact, a declaration of sickness over my life. The universe and all of Heaven and earth respond to our words and our confessions. It's time to stop even speaking of your marriage in the same way you always have. Heaven is listening, and by divine design the universe is giving you exactly what you are confessing over your marriage and your spouse. When engaged or married couples come to me for training, seeming to find themselves battling all-out war, more times than not, the confusion has arisen because of the confessions and the affirmations that have been made over the marriage. Though they haven't realized it fully, the partners had become their own worst enemy within the marriage. Even though they may have confessed that they wanted healing or a sense of renewed intimacy and trust, their very own words and affirmations had been contradicting their own confessions. The Book of James teaches us that double-minded people shouldn't even expect to receive anything from GOD. Yes, double-mindedness is literally a catastrophic danger.

If you truly want to reconcile your marriage and find a greater sense of intimacy with your spouse, it's time to begin affirming the good again. It's time to begin honoring the qualities and the characteristics of your spouse that are wonderful and attractive. Stop speaking to your friends about your marriage if the conversations will paint your spouse in a negative light. Heaven is listening and the universe is taking note of every idle word to create even more of your confession. If you truly want to bring healing into your home once again, the answer lies within your very own thought life – within your very own perspective. Deep within you, even now, resides all the power of the Godhead, bodily. You are a creator, by divine, intelligent design. Your very words and your very thoughts – your intentions – are continuously signaling to the universe and to all of Heaven and earth the true contents of your own heart. It's time to reassess your mindset and your own thought life. Rather than simply reacting, begin to recognize that, yes, you do have a choice in how you respond and rather than responding from the place of negativity and anger, choose, instead, to respond from the place of creative, attractive power. When you begin to do this, I assure you, you will begin to see the miracle of transformation taking place within your own marriage, within the life of your spouse, but, above all, within your very own life.

# JOINED TOGETHER

*"What you affirm, you will continue to manifest." – Jeremy Lopez*

When I hear individuals profess to be "Christian," I must admit that the declarations mean very little to me. In fact, in total and complete transparency and authenticity, such statements and declarations are worthless to me. Words mean very little when attempting to capture or define identity. Show me action. Actions reveal the reality of intentions and motives. Perhaps you've heard these statements as well from various individuals in your own life. "My doctor is a Christian." "I chose the attorney because he's a Christian." "I shop at her store because she goes to my church." So, what? What sort of qualifications does the doctor have? How many cases has the attorney successfully litigated in court? What is the quality of the product offered in your friend's store? You see, so often we place such emphasis on being "Christian" that we lose sight of our own true intentions, our own motives, and the content of our own character. As a result, our relationships fall into disarray and our marriages suffer as we place emphasis on religion over reality. Today, within your marriage to your difficult spouse, you are creating a reality, moment by moment and day by day, with each passing thought you have.

There's an old, religious adage which says, "The road to Hell is paved with good intentions." The problem, though, is that it simply isn't true. It's neither scripturally accurate nor theologically sound. Understanding intention paves the way to the miracles of the inner Kingdom of Heaven which

Jesus taught and spoke of, because the universe responds solely to the energy of intention. Religion has always had a way of looking on the outward, rather than the inward – looking at the actions of individuals rather than the content of the heart. Often times, we are guilty of bringing this same, religious programming into our marriages. When I speak of programming, I'm referring to the premise of our own expectations.

Now I'm in no way saying that you should ever, in any way, lower your expectations of your own marriage. However, what I am saying, though, is that when your spouse fails to live up to your own expectations of him or her, you're going to be given a very divine choice. You will either condemn and judge; or you will choose, instead, to see the good. That choice will be yours and yours alone, and the impetus of responsibility will rest solely upon your own shoulders, regardless of what your spouse does. Remember, my friend, your reaction is a choice you consciously choose to make and not some reflexive, triggered response of which you have no control over. Within the rule and reign of the inner Kingdom of Heaven which Jesus spoke of, you possess all power and all dominion over your emotions and over your responses. That's why Jesus continually taught that the Kingdom of Heaven is *within*. He was speaking, in fact, of the inner person with its emotions and its will and its thoughts. The power behind the Biblical Law of Attraction rests solely upon one's ability to get in touch with their own, true intention and true will. The universe and all of Heaven and earth are constantly and continuously asking, "What do you truly want to create?" Your response to that question comes from the thoughts you think, the emotions you harbor, and the actions you show. In other words, your marriage is truly being built upon the bedrock of your own intention. And for this reason, it's time to reassess your own motives, your own thoughts, and your very own intention if you are ever going to truly bring healing and balance back into your home and into your love affair once again.

Whether you've realized it, consciously, yet or not, you are the single greatest contributing factor to the outcome of your marriage – not your difficult spouse. Remember, you and only you are responsible for your own energy, your own thoughts, and your own intention. In other words, you are responsible for your reactions to difficult moments. Knowing that, because of the powerful principle of the Biblical Law of Attraction, you are continuously creating and attracting into your life and into your marriage based upon your thoughts, it's time that you begin to recognize much more fully the powerful principle of the marriage covenant. Although you, individually, possess the creative and attractive power of the Godhead and possess the divine ability to create and recreate your life based upon your own thoughts and perception, something truly heavenly and magical takes place the moment that you make the choice to enter into a covenantal agreement with another person. By exchanging vows and making promises to each other before GOD, you and your spouse have come into alignment. Although you do possess your own unique and individual thoughts and possess the ability to make your own decisions based upon your own individual will, you and your spouse have become singularly and irrevocably "one" in the sight of all of Heaven and earth. Promises have been made. A vision has been cast. By choosing to enter into the covenantal agreement of the marriage bond, you have been spiritually and energetically "joined" to another and a divine merging has taken place within the Kingdom of Heaven. Does this mean that you are no longer capable of having your own thoughts and your own will? Absolutely not. What this does mean, though, is that based upon the heavenly principles of partnership and covenantal agreement, you are no longer acting, solely, upon your own unique individuality.

This precedent was established by the Creator in the very beginning within the garden paradise and decreed by Him. We find this heavenly declaration in the very beginning of the scriptures, set forth within the Book of Genesis. *"Therefore shall a man leave his father and his mother, and shall cleave unto his wife: and they shall be one flesh." (Genesis 2:24 KJV)* With this declaration, the Creator was establishing the most powerful covenantal agreement of all – the agreement of divine union and partnership. You've, I'm sure, heard the "blessing" often pronounced in marriage ceremonies which says, "What GOD has joined together let no man put asunder." This blessing depicts the importance and the permanence of the divine union of marriage. Marriage, my friend, is much, much more than just an agreed upon decision. It's much more than simply a trial run or some experiment in which both individuals simply hope for the best. No. It is, rather, a sacred and solemn contract with the universe – an agreement which the universe recognizes and which all of Heaven takes notice of. Throughout my years of prophetic coaching, I've so often heard many individuals exclaim that their marriages simply weren't working. This simply isn't true, though, based upon the Biblical Law of Attraction. When someone says, "My marriage is no longer working," what they are, in fact, saying is, "*I'm* no longer willing to do the work."

Marriage, as a divine covenant, is a solemn oath which is established and recorded in Heaven and manifested within the earth. Although it may not seem like it in the heated and often chaotic moments of marriage with your "difficult" spouse, Heaven recognizes your union and sees the two of you as one, individual, energetic union and no longer as two, distinct individuals, based upon the scriptures. So, knowing this, the all-important and all-powerful question is, "What are you doing to solidify the energy of your marriage, based upon your thoughts?" All too often, the term "marriage" is relegated to nothing more than just a piece of paper in today's modern culture – particularly here in westernized society. However, nothing could be further from the truth. Marriage is a blending – both spiritually and physically – a merging into one, joined identity. As uncomfortable as it may be to recognize, by exchanging vows, you have forfeited your right to disrespect your spouse and have given up all claims to your own right to bring toxicity and negativity into your home. The moment you begin to recognize your solemn vow in this way, I assure you, you will begin to be much, much more cognizant of your actions, your words, and your intent. The marriage oath should and must always be taken seriously.

Now I'm in no way seeking to suggest that in order to have a truly successful and happy marriage union that you have to be some sort of wallflower, incapable of having your own voice and your own thoughts. What I am saying, though, is that upon entering into the sacred and solemn vows of the marriage covenant, the universe no longer recognizes you and your spouse as two, separate and distinct voices but, rather, as one unified "energy." Heaven recognizes partnership and agreement above all else. Jesus, himself, taught us this powerful principle of agreement throughout his earthly ministry. *"Again I say unto you, That if two of you shall agree on earth as touching any thing that they shall ask, it shall be done for them of my Father which is in heaven." (Matthew 18:19 KJV)* I often cannot help but think that as Jesus spoke these words, the idea of the marriage covenant was on his mind. By being "joined" together, you have, in essence, amplified exponentially the creative and attractive power which you've always possessed, multiplying it by two. For this reason, the chaos and the moments of difficulty which you choose to dwell upon concerning your marriage is magnified, recreated, and continuously manifested a hundredfold. Again, what you affirm you will continue to manifest – particularly within the covenant of marriage. From a much, much more practical perspective, this means that when you choose to dwell upon the negative and unseemly qualities of your spouse, you are literally signaling to the universe that you, yourself, are exhibiting and exuding those same, exact qualities. In other words, by choosing to affirm the negative and all of those things you don't want, you're literally becoming the very thing you claim to despise.

The universe and the entire Kingdom of Heaven operates continuously from the perspective of the "NOW." I will share more on this powerful principle of the "present" in a moment; however, concerning the power of becoming joined together, I want to encourage you to begin to see that regardless of past moments and regardless of any fears or anxiety concerning the future of your marriage, the way that you are now choosing to see and to view your marriage and your spouse in this exact moment – this "NOW" moment – is the way the universe and all of Heaven and earth are currently seeing you. This is the important and all-powerful perspective of a covenantal agreement. Though you, individually, possess great power with your own thoughts and intention, Heaven and earth are viewing the force of your thoughts in an even more amplified and magnified way. Concerning the agreement of marriage, truly, the two have become one flesh in the eyes of the Holy Spirit.

# THE JOINT SUPPLIES

Recently, for a prophetic teaching I did for the readers, subscribers, partners, and students of Identity Network, I wrote an article entitled *Every Joint Supplies*. In truth, the prophetic word was not simply a call for unity within the Body of Christ but, even more so, a call to recognize the all-important principle of agreement and partnership. When we think of the principle of partnership, we are reminded not only of the role that we, as individuals, are to play but also the role that two individuals who have chosen to come into agreement together play. It simply cannot be stated enough, my friend, that Heaven takes the concepts of divine union and attractive partnerships quite, quite seriously indeed. In his epistles to the early church, the Apostle Paul spoke of the power of partnerships by describing them as "joints" within the body. In his epistle to the church at Ephesus, Paul writes, *"From whom the whole body fitly joined together and compacted by that which every joint supplieth, according to the effectual working in the measure of every part, maketh increase of the body unto the edifying of itself in love."* (Ephesians 4:16 KJV) In this passage, we are reminded not only of the all-important power of partnership but also of the principle of diversity.

Every person has a very unique and important role to play. This is perhaps never any more true than when viewed within the context of the marriage covenant. Whether you realize it or not, by being "joined," you and your spouse have entered into an agreement that is supplying the energy of literally every aspect of life. As we've discussed, the moment you and your partner made the conscious and willing choice to enter into covenantal agreement, the two of you became one in the sight of Heaven. However, to better understand this, within the context of Paul's writing to the early church, you must recognize fully that it is the joining, itself, which is creating literally everything you are now experiencing. As Paul states, the "joint supplies." This is a great and all-important reminder that, as a married person, the union of marriage, itself, is not only beneficial to you but that it is now your greatest asset and a strength rather than a liability or as some difficulty which must be overcome. It's time, my friend, to begin to see your marriage from the eyes of the Kingdom, if you are ever going to be fully healed. Knowing that the joint supplies all needs, recognize that your partnership and your union with your spouse is, in fact, serving a far greater purpose for you than you may have ever realized before.

Often, within the church, we are reminded of just how important it is to have someone to "do life" with. However, the marriage union is not simply two individuals choosing to "do life" together but is, rather, an energetic and symbiotic union that is formed. Once energy begins to be established, it can be very difficult to change – especially when the energy is being amplified and magnified by two people. Allow me to give you an example of this truth. Often, when two individuals are dating or even become engaged, the arguments and the disagreements over differences can seem quite trivial at first. However, once the vows of marriage are made before GOD, the disagreements that once seemed so minor, insignificant, and trivial, suddenly become much more amplified. This, alone, is a reminder of the power of covenant.

It's also part of the reason things can seem so very different once the vows of marriage are taken. The truth of the matter is that things *are* different for you now. No longer are you simply an individual who wishes to date or to even be engaged to another individual; you are now one flesh with your spouse. Recognizing the power of this divine partnership of being "joined" together must now serve as a reminder to begin to view your marriage much, much differently than you have been. Remember, it is your perspective and your thoughts – what you are choosing to affirm – which is fueling what you are continuing to manifest within your home.

I remember, now looking back, a time when I once coached a young, married couple who had come to Identity Network for insight into their love affair. Having been married for only a few months, the young couple was still, quite literally enjoying the bliss that so often accompanies the "honeymoon" phase of any marriage bond. Well, at least, that's what *should* have been happening. Everything seemed to be going perfectly for the young couple from the moment they had first met while in college. They never seemed to have even the slightest disagreement over anything. Communication flourished, and everything seemed much like a fun and enjoyable adventure shared between two best friends. Then, though, vows were exchanged. Within only a matter of weeks following the marriage ceremony, it seemed as though literally everything had begun to change. Two individuals had been energetically joined as one. As they came to me, they expressed, "Jeremy, it's as if the moment we exchanged vows, everything changed. Things seem so much more serious now." The young woman, Shelly, expressed to me, "Now, even the things that once seemed so minor and insignificant quickly escalate into arguments and heated fights." The truth of the matter, though, is that things *had* changed. Two individuals had been joined together as one flesh and their energies were now being amplified and magnified exponentially. I shared with them the principles of the Biblical Law of Attraction, explaining how, now being joined together, the covenantal agreement was serving as a magnifying glass, heightening their true intentions and their deepest thoughts.

You see, it's possible to hide your true identity in a dating relationship. It's even possible to hide your true feelings while being engaged. It's not possible, however, to hide within a marriage covenant, because the universe will demand your complete authenticity. For this reason, things can so quickly seem to change for couples once the vows of marriage are exchanged and promises to honor are made. Again, the universe takes the symbiotic and energetic union of covenant quite seriously. I explained to the young couple that what most consider to

be the "honeymoon" phase of the marriage is actually a phase which requires the work of introspection and self-acknowledgement. In truth, there is no phase of a marriage partnership which doesn't require the element of work and soul searching. Transparency and authenticity are essential to the union of marriage, and this is why it is so vitally important to know yourself and to know the power of your own thoughts long, long before ever even entertaining the idea of entering into marriage.

Often, much of the confusion surrounding difficult marriages stems from a lack of self-awareness. How can you truly know and be able to relate to another individual when you haven't fully understood your true self? Marriage will demand that the masks be removed. The energy of the Biblical Law of Attraction at work within a marriage forces transparency and authenticity. It demands personal responsibility. Far, far too often, we view the concept of marriage from the premise that it is simply just another relationship we form within the journey of life. This, though, is not the case at all. By recognizing that your life and your marriage is being fueled and created by the "joining" that has taken place and recognizing that the energy of your experiences are now much, much more heightened and amplified through the magnifying lens of covenant, it's now more important than at any time to begin to relate to your spouse from the place of honor.

Recognize that your spouse has qualities that are unique to him or her. The scriptures make it plain that Christ is the head of all things and that all things – literally *all* things – are in Him and by Him and for Him, for the purpose of His own good pleasure and the accomplishing of His own will. Knowing this, how can you judge the qualities and the characteristics of your spouse when he or she doesn't seem to meet your expectations? My friend, you are setting yourself up for failure if you are unwilling to view your spouse from a more spiritual perspective and if you choose to view him or her from your own desire to control. The joining which takes places when two individuals enter into a covenantal agreement is much more than just a relationship; it is a divine union and a blending of soul energies – forcing two to become one flesh.

What you choose to say about your marriage or about your spouse, whether good or bad, you are saying about your own self. Your spouse is an extension of your own identity now – like it or not – and there is no escaping it. When you share with your friends or with your extended family or with your coworkers how lazy or how unattractive or how unreliable your spouse is, you are actually saying much, much more about your own self than you are of him or her. For those who truly know me well, they know that I am very protective of my own energy and my own inner circle. When someone begins to speak negatively of their spouse to me, before telling them I don't want to engage in negativity, I often cannot help but think to myself, "Well, why did you marry them?" It can be described as human nature, our incessant nature to judge and to critique those things which we don't like. However, marriage is a spiritual force within Heaven and earth and, when speaking of the Biblical Law of Attraction, we are, inadvertently, also speaking of the universal Law of Cause and Effect and the Law of Sowing and Reaping. What you place into your marriage is what you will continue to manifest for your marriage and also for your very own life. What you speak of concerning your marriage, you are attracting to yourself and into the life of your partner. What you think of concerning your marriage, you are, in fact, saying to the universe, "I desire more of this." It's time to begin to recognize the all-powerful nature of your "joint" identity now that you are within a marriage bond.

People find it disturbing, often, when I say to them that there are no secrets in marriage. You may be thinking, "Jeremy, that can't possibly be true because there are *still* things I've never shared with my husband." It doesn't matter.

What you've verbally chosen to withhold is completely and absolutely irrelevant. The karmic effect of sowing and reaping is still in full effect within your marriage and within your life and what you've chosen to withhold may not surface in the form of a conversation with your spouse; however, rest assured it absolutely will surface in the form of your spouse keeping his or her own secrets from you and living a more secretive life. You see, there is no escaping the Law of Attraction. It is a universal law and a divine and spiritual principle of existence. When you withhold or attempt to hide something from your spouse, thinking that he or she will never find out about it, you are only hurting yourself. By sowing deception and disrespect, you will be forced to face even more deception and even more disrespect. This is why it is so vitally important that you begin to become much more aware of the role that you are playing within the union of marriage.

In truth, from the spiritual perspective of the Kingdom of Heaven, there truly is one singular identity within the bond of marriage; there is only union and one, singular energy manifesting itself through symbiotic partnership. The universe and all of Heaven is demanding total and complete authenticity and absolute devotion to the work of partnership. This is often times where the concept of "mirroring" begins to manifest. When a husband or wife intentionally withholds information or attempt to deceive or manipulate the other, the partner, in turn, begins to exhibit those same tendencies, often without ever even consciously realizing it. Marriage is energy, just as all things in existence are. A simple science lesson from third grade reminds us of this. Although the form may change, the substance remains the same. What you are putting into your marriage is exactly what you are continuing to experience. You will breed what you continue to dwell upon. It always begins in the smallest, most seemingly insignificant of ways – with open doors.

# OPEN DOORS

*"Disrespect is a cancer to your marriage." –*
*Jeremy Lopez*

The very moment you first open the door to disrespect in our marriage, you are allowing a literal cancer to begin to grow. The scriptures declare *"A little leaven leaveneth the whole lump." (Galatians 5:9 KJV)* In other words, the very moment even the smallest dose of what you don't want is introduced, the very thing you don't want will continue to spread. I felt led to include within this book a chapter on the power of open doors within your marriage. Whether you realize it yet or not, consciously, there are doors that are opened which you, yourself, have opened without ever even being fully aware of it. These open doors have remained open because of your own thoughts, your own words, and the intentions of your own heart. I know you're probably thinking, "But Jeremy what about the doors that my difficult spouse has opened?" I'm sure, by now, you've realized that the only person who can be responsible for your reactions to your spouse is, in fact, your very own self. No one else is capable of controlling and managing your emotions except for you.

With the creative and powerful force of the Biblical Law of Attraction comes, also, the role of personal responsibility. Often times the most detrimental and most catastrophic of breaking points begin with even the smallest, seemingly most insignificant actions and thoughts. From there – from one open door – the issue builds and the thought life begins to run rampant, taking on a life of its own. Before long, what began as a small, open door becomes a floodgate as pent up emotions and repressed feelings flow toward the surface. Hateful, rage-filled words ensue, along with an even stronger desire to control. Allow me to explain by sharing a few practical examples from actual clients.

"It didn't seem like a very big deal, so I didn't tell my husband I had been texting my old, high school crush." "I used my own money, so I didn't tell my wife about the purchase." "I have my own life, and so when I decided to spend a weekend out with my girlfriends, I didn't even give my husband a chance to interject." "Together, my husband and I own a business, but when we disagree on business plans, I always get my own way." "I decided to grab drinks with a few buddies after work. I provide for the family so it doesn't matter if my wife approves or not." In more than twenty years of prophetic coaching, I've heard it all before. But for every "I didn't think it would be a big deal" and "It was none of his business" I've heard twice as many "I couldn't control myself and the affair just happened" and "We've decided to get a divorce." You see, what so often may seem quite insignificant and inconsequential can often lead to moments of absolute catastrophe. I want to share with you something that you may not have ever considered before: emotional catastrophes within marriages are always, always, always premeditated, whether we like to admit that or not. And they always begin, at first, with a small, open door.

The moment you begin to open a doorway to disrespect and secrecy within your marriage, you are inviting catastrophe and regardless of your desire to change, catastrophe will always ensue after the seeds of chaos have been planted. It all begins, first, within the thought life of an individual. As you now know and as I have shared, all elements of life stem from the thoughts within – from the mind, the will, and the emotions. Proverbs makes it quite clear that what we think, we are. By bringing into the marriage union even the slightest element of disrespect, you are contributing to the energy of confusion which you claim to not want. Over the years, as I've had the privilege and honor of coaching literally thousands of couples within their marriages, my heart has often become broken as I've witnessed the deterioration of foundations time and time again, for no other reason than that doors were opened allowing seeds of chaos to be planted. It always begins innocently enough, though. With simply, "It doesn't matter" or "He'll not really mind." More times than not, though, it's "He can't tell me what to do" or "She can have her opinion, but I'm my own person." All things stem from the innermost depths of the heart and mind. From our words to our very actions, everything stems from within. We've spoken of the eternal and transcendent principle of being "joined" together, energetically, in the eyes of Heaven; however, the passage of scripture I shared depicting how every joint supplies isn't the only time we find the analogy of "joints" within the New Testament.

Although the Apostle Paul spoke of the importance of recognizing the role of "joints" being fit tightly together into a working union, the writer of Hebrews also uses the analogy to depict the deeper and innermost aspects of one's own innermost being. *"For the word of God is quick, and powerful, and sharper than any twoedged sword, piercing even to the dividing asunder of soul and spirit, and of the joints and marrow, and is a discerner of the thoughts and intents of the heart." (Hebrews 4:12 KJV)* In this passage of scripture, the writer of Hebrews uses the analogy of joints and morrow to depict the hidden and innermost thoughts and intentions of one's heart. My friend, it's time to take a deeper and more intimate look at your very own self and to recognize your very own intentions and thoughts if you are ever going to begin to exude the energy of harmony within your marriage bond. It's time to stop looking simply upon the surface and upon the outward actions of your spouse and begin to recognize that what you are seeing is but a mirror of your very own intentions and thoughts. *This* is the core foundation of the Biblical Law of Attraction. Your very own thoughts are manifesting before your very eyes in the form of your spouse, and rather than recognizing the contributing role that you've been playing all along, you've chosen, instead, to cast blame and to fuel even more negativity and resentment and chaos.

Negativity breeds more negativity. Anger and the desire to control breed only more of the same. Today, I want to encourage you to begin to ask yourself, "What am I contributing to the difficulties I've complained about for so long?" Now, although at first glance I'm sure you'd love to give a very dismissive response and cast blame entirely upon your difficult spouse, the truth of the matter is that the Biblical Law of Attraction says otherwise. The universe is asking you to look at your own reflection in the mirror and to see, as uncomfortable as it might seem at first, that you are contributing to the very things you claim to despise by allowing certain doors to remain open within your own thought life. The scriptures make it quite plain that everything stems from within, and whether you refer to is karmic law or as the result of the

Law of Sowing and Reaping, what you plant within your marriage through the doors you choose to open will come back upon you and upon your spouse in the most exponential of ways. *"As I have observed, those who plow evil and those who sow trouble reap it." (Job 4:8 KJV)* *"So in everything, do to others what you would have them do to you, for this sums up the Law and the Prophets." (Matthew 7:12 KJV)* *"Whoever seeks good finds favor, but evil comes to one who searches for it." (Proverbs 11:27 KJV)* As you can see, throughout the entirety of the scriptures, one can see the Law of Attraction in full operation. What we give, we bring back upon ourselves. This is especially true in covenantal partnerships. What you allow into your marriage bond will continue to manifest and to grow.

For decades, I've taught the secrets of the Biblical Law of Attraction. When the Holy

Spirit opened my spiritual eyes to the truth behind the principle, it changed my life in an astounding and transcendent way. By beginning to implement the principle of attraction into my own, personal life, I began to see the miracle of attraction at work. By becoming more aware of the role that I play within my own life and by affirming what I truly do want rather than what I don't, I began to see success in literally every area of my life. As I shared within my book *Creating with Your Thoughts*, the moment you begin to recognize your own self as a co-creator with GOD and as the visionary and architect of your life experiences based upon your thoughts, everything will begin to change in an instant. You and I are continuously being given the opportunity to reassess, recalibrate, and, in turn, recreate the lives of our dreams. The principle works in all areas of business, all areas of success building, as it creates wealth, and it harnesses the inner drive to create. Far, far too often, though, we fail to realize this principle of creative attraction is also at work with the people in our lives – all of our relationships. Often times, we forget just how intricate a role the mind and thought forms play in our dealings with other people. By failing to see this, we begin to create carelessly and haphazardly, becoming casual and flippant with our words, our thoughts, and our actions. My friend, I want to make you yet another promise. If you would become as thoughtful in your marriage as you are in matters of business, you will see a transformative change within the atmosphere of your union. If you would think as clearly of the words you use when speaking to your spouse as you do when speaking with your own clients or with others dear to you, you would see the unwanted open doors begin to close. If you would focus as intently upon the energy you place into your covenantal agreement of marriage as you do upon your own desires and the harnessing of your own, individual will, gone would be the days of living with the element of chaos and confusion in your home. The choice, though, is completely yours.

When I released my best-selling book *Attracting Your Godly Spouse*, I shared how the principle of creative attraction plays a critical role in our interactions with other people. I included, even, a chapter entitled "Attraction 101" in which I shared how the chemistry and attraction we feel with certain people is actually not a physical reaction but, rather, a spiritual one. Even the attraction you once felt toward your spouse stemmed from your own, inner thought. Well, it's time to begin to reassess, recalibrate, and begin to recreate a new and more healthy marriage union by getting in touch with your own creative, attractive power once again. It's time to become more thoughtful of your own role within the union. Chances are, as you now find yourself reading these words, unwanted doors have been opened within your marriage – doors through which unwanted seeds of negativity and malice have been sown. As I've said before, it takes two to tango, so although your spouse has played a very real role in the matter and you aren't solely responsible for the chaos and the heartbreak that you're now experiencing, you are, solely, responsible for the recreation of your own life and your own energy. By the divine and intelligent design of a caring and loving, all-powerful Creator, you and I are infused with the transcendent power of Creation. With our thoughts and with the understanding of our own, true will, we create. However, the same power by which we create is also the same power by which we can recreate and begin to build anew all over again. I want to encourage you, in closing this chapter, to begin to learn to recognize the role you, yourself, have played in keeping unwanted doors open. As difficult and as seemingly unattractive the actions of your spouse, the truth is that you have had a role to play as well.

Take responsibility for your own role and for the doors that you have continued to allow to remain open, based upon your own actions, thoughts, and intention. It truly is a universal and heavenly principle from which there is no escaping. Your thoughts are the basis of all of your experiences – both within the public life of your career and also within the private life of your marriage. It's time to begin to reassess the role you've played. By doing so, only then will you be able to recreate a more balanced and more prosperous union of marriage with your spouse. Again, what you affirm, you will continue to manifest. Just as the scriptures declare, *"Whoever seeks good finds favor, but evil comes to one who searches for it,"* you are being reminded today that in order to create more of the "good," you must, first of all, begin to see more of the "good." By dwelling upon the negativity and the difficulty, you are only signaling to the universe and to all of Heaven and earth that you desire more of such things. Even in the most tumultuous and most chaotic moments of marriage, the change begins with you.

# THE NOW MOMENT

*"Begin to bring the power of 'NOW' into your marriage." – Jeremy Lopez*

As I write these words to you and as I look back, it was nearly a decade ago now that my best-selling book *The Power of the Eternal Now* was first released to a global audience. It instantly became a best-seller, due to the power of the Holy Spirit and also due to the principle of the Biblical Law of Attraction. To this day, I still receive testimony after testimony from individuals throughout the world whose lives were changed by the principles contained within that book. When the Holy Spirit first began to birth within me the premise of the book, I heard the voice of the LORD speak to me concerning the power of "NOW" moments. Within the

Kingdom of Heaven, there is only the present now. In fact, the writer of the Book of Hebrews declares that "NOW" faith is the substance of things hoped for and the evidence of things not seen. In other words, the Kingdom of Heaven which Jesus continually spoke of and taught is a realm and a domain in which we are continuously being driven to recognize our power of creative force within each moment. In order to do this, though, we must refuse to surrender to the mindset which causes us to feel like victims of our past, all while also abandoning the anxiety and the fear of the future. In other words, in order to prosper within the Kingdom of Heaven and in order to truly begin to master your own creative, attractive power, you're going to have to first master the art of being truly present in the moment of "now."

Throughout the years, as marriage couples have come to me to inquire for their marriages the Word of the LORD, all too often I have found that much of the confusion and the heartbreak that arises within the unions of marriage do so because one or both partners have failed to recognize the importance of being present, within the now moment. As visual beings, created by GOD with the ability to cast vision and to dream, you are also given the ability to look back and to look forward. Though this divine, heavenly gift of sight is truly a blessing, all too often, depending upon the intention we place into our sight, we can either move from the guilt of the past or to the anxiety which can, at times, surround thoughts of the future. Somewhere in-between, though, amidst all of the emotion of guilt and uncertainty, there is an even more heavenly perspective and a more powerful state of being –

the moment of the present. I felt led to include this chapter as a way to inspire you to recognize just how much power you have right now – today – in this eternal, now moment. Although life is but a series of moments, each passing moment is eternal because of the force of creation we place within it with each passing thought. Today, for instance, is the direct result of yesterday's thoughts, actions, and intentions. This morning, as you rose from bed to greet the new day, you were quite literally stepping into an experience of life that you have created based upon the thoughts of the past. The home you now reside in stems from the inspiration of days gone by. The career you enjoy each day is the direct result of planning and thoughts of yesteryear. In other words, the life you now enjoy each day exists as it does based solely upon your own plans, your own past thoughts, and your own creative, attractive force. The same is true, also, of your marriage. The marriage bond you now experience each day is the direct result of your own thoughts from the past, your own attractive power which drew your spouse into your life, and also, more importantly, a decision that you willingly and willfully chose to make. Regardless of the current atmosphere of your home and regardless of the state of the marriage, currently, your marriage is something that at one time you had prayed for, visualized, and consciously wanted.

To better understand the important, all-powerful principle of the now moment, one must first begin to grapple with the idea of time. Time can be quite the elusive concept, though, considering how linear time here within our world is an idea confined solely to our natural world. There is no time within the Kingdom of Heaven. In fact, there is no passing of time. The Kingdom of Heaven within is an ageless and timeless realm, existing apart from the confines of calendars, dates, and anniversary celebrations. *"But, beloved, be not ignorant of this one thing, that one day is with the Lord as a thousand years, and a thousand years as one day." (2 Peter 3:8 KJV)* Although the element of time is insignificant within the eternal realm of the inner Kingdom within, the consideration of time is important to the natural, human perspective. In other words, here within our world of natural physicality, anniversaries matter. Birthdays and holidays are celebrated. In fact, imagine not recognizing the anniversary of your marriage or the birthday of your spouse. And when your partner asks why you'd forgotten simply telling them that "time" doesn't matter. Someone would be forced to sleep on the couch, I assure you. You see, to us, here within the natural world, we view time much differently than Heaven does because, here, we see so clearly the effects of time passing. We see aging. We see the deterioration of things. Even more importantly, though, we possess memories of moments long since passed. These memories of ours serve as constant reminders that we have experienced life through very memorable moments of existence. Too, as we think toward the future, we also recognize, instinctively, that there will soon come other moments, as well. Tomorrow there will be even more to experience, to enjoy, to love, and to process through. Yes, indeed, time, as we consider time, matters greatly to us.

The old adage really is true, though. There truly is no time quite like the present moment. If you were to begin to consider time in much more of an eternal way, I promise you that you'd begin to become much, much more aware of what you're contributing to each and every moment of life. So often, particularly within the marriage relationship, we choose, by willing choice, either to dwell upon past moments or to look toward some future experience we hope will one day arrive. As we visualize, both the past and the future, emotions become activated as we see the images of life flash before us, as a film upon a movie screen. As these emotions become activated, we often either long for the past or we, rather, regret it deeply. I so often say that regret is simply a reminder of lessons we failed to learn in past moments. With regret comes the guilt which can so often plague us. Then, as we look toward the future and process through our own visions of what we hope we will one day experience, a sense of anxiety begins to arise within us, often times shaking us to our core. In-between it all, though, there is peace within the present moment of existence – within the now moment. This peace is a reminder from the Kingdom of Heaven that we are being given a choice of how we wish to create. In each present moment, the voice of the Holy Spirit – that inner voice of the Kingdom of Heaven within – asks, "What do you truly want?" As thoughts pass, creation is enacted all over again. This is the powerful and heavenly beauty of visualization. Though we can choose to be haunted by our pasts or plagued with anxiety over future uncertainties, we are always, always creating something.

We choose, by conscious, willing choice, which thoughts we dwell upon. By choice, we choose to dwell upon the moments of the past, thoughts of the future, or upon the present moment. When we bring our thoughts of the past into the marriage union, we open a door for the seeds of turmoil to be planted. Allow me to share with you a practical example of this. Once, years ago, while ministering to a married couple from Los Angeles, I sensed by the Holy

Spirit that both partners had become trapped within the moments of the past. Speaking of something that had happened years prior, the wife said to me, "I just can't seem to let it go. Even though he lied to me two years ago, it still seems like only yesterday." In response, her husband expressed genuine remorse for his actions – a remorse that he had been exhibiting for two years. Together, their message to me was consistent. "We just can't keep going on this way." The truth of the matter, though, is that they were both correct. They couldn't continue to dwell upon the sins of the past because, for them, the past had continuously, daily been brought into the present moment. As I listened to them intently, my heart went out to them as I sensed the heartbreak and anger from her as well as the exhaustion from him. "I can't keep trying to prove myself to her," he exclaimed. "I'm not the person I used to be."

As they spoke, with tears in their eyes, I heard the voice of the LORD say to me, "They are both prisoners of the past, but this is a new moment." Instinctively, as I heard the voice of the LORD come to me, I knew that a decision was being asked of them both. The universe and all of Heaven was requiring that they enact change – regardless of the decision. As we battle the emotions of the past which we allow to linger, we often forget that time within our world continues to pass. Suddenly, in what seems like the blinking of an eye, two years pass. Heaven, for the couple, was asking that a decision to move forward be made. Their decision, regardless of the outcome, would serve only to free them both.

Then, there is the story of Michael and Angela, a young couple I had the privilege of meeting just after the release of my book *Attracting Your Godly Spouse*. As I met them while on a book tour, I noticed that the beautiful, young couple before me seemed to be plagued by an overwhelming sense of anxiety. It was obvious to me. The couple had just become engaged after nearly four years of a dating relationship. The moment Michael asked Angela to marry him, she immediately and without hesitation said, "Of course." Then came the fear, though. Some of the fear being understandable and some being completely irrational, all of the fear had become tormenting for them both. "Jeremy, will we still be together twenty years from now?" "Will he still love me even when we're older?" As I looked upon their young, beautiful faces, it was obvious to me that, unlike the prior example where a marriage was plagued by the past, Michael and Angela were both being tormented by lingering thoughts of the future and questions regarding what would be. As Angela asked her question, I heard the voice of the LORD say so very clearly, "You have been given *this* moment to create with."

You see, my friend, from the perspective of the heavenly and all-powerful realm of the inner Kingdom of Heaven, there is only the now – only the present. The harsh and seemingly brutal reality is that you do not have the right to hold the past over the head of your spouse, regardless of what those past moments may or may not have entailed. It's unfair, and it's wrong. Sure, although you claim that you have forgiven him the sins of the past, the very fact that, now, all these years later, you continue to bring it us, shows that you're lying to yourself and to the world. Am I suggesting that you should forget? No. In fact, to even attempt to try and forget the past is a futile move, as memories exist to fuel our testimonies. However, you were never destined to dwell in your past moments. You are being given the choice, today, to begin anew. You are also the only person responsible for the creation of your own future life. In Matthew 6:34, Jesus declares, *"Take therefore no thought for the morrow: for the morrow shall take thought for the things of itself. Sufficient unto the day is the evil thereof."* In other words, more plainly put, to continue to worry about the uncertainties of tomorrow is to ensure that when tomorrow comes, the worry will continue to plague you.

Today, I want you to lovingly and prayerfully encourage you to begin to become much, much more present in your marriage than ever before. Not only because you deserve to be free from the chains of the past and from the fear of the future but because your spouse deserves that freedom and liberation as well. It's unfair to your spouse, in fact, for you to fail to be present. It is always within the present moment – within the "NOW" moment of existence – that you and your spouse are able to create and to begin to recreate. The past cannot be changed. Did it hurt and was the pain unbearable? Yes. I admit that. Is the fear of the future a fear which seems very real to you? Yes. However, you are only able to create from the perspective of the now. *"Whereas ye know not what shall be on the morrow. For what is your life? It is even a vapour, that appeareth for a little time, and then vanisheth away." (James 4:14 KJV)* In this passage from the Book of James, we are shown what is, perhaps, the most telling of all scriptures detailing the importance of learning to be more present in each and every moment of existence. The scripture compares life to a vapor, which passes away and vanishes before our natural eyesight. It is so true, though, if you think about it. I'm sure that, right now, it may seem like only yesterday when you enjoyed your wedding day. It, perhaps, seems like only yesterday when your first child was born. Now, years have passed before your eyes. Time has passed. It's slipped away. I want to encourage you, though, by offering to you the prophetic and universal truth that in this very moment – *this* moment – you are being given the opportunity to integrate into the story of your life literally every past moment as a way to heal and become more whole and complete. Although the moments of the past have now slipped away into the eternal and though the thought of the future brings with it a sense of uncertainty, you still have this moment – this eternal now moment. And the Holy Spirit and the Kingdom of Heaven are even now continuing to ask you, lovingly, "What do you want to create?" My friend, there's still time and there's still hope. You can create your marriage anew and afresh in *this* moment. This moment, like all moments, will last forever. Use it wisely.

# MIRRORING

*"You see your spouse the way you see your very own self." – Jeremy Lopez*

All those years ago, when I was first awakened to the immense, transcendent power of the principle of Biblical, Kingdom attraction, I must admit, the reality of such a power seemed overwhelming to me at first. To even begin to understand the premise of the Biblical Law of Attraction seemed quite the daunting task. What did it all mean? Prophetically, throughout my years in ministry, I had been so familiar with the Law of Sowing and Reaping, as well as the principle of seed-time and harvest. However, this was something else entirely. The principle of creative attraction, it seemed, went far beyond simply being able to reap what I had sown. It became clear that creative attraction, established in the very beginning, went far, far beyond just wishful thinking and a desire to exude a sense of positivity. No. It was far more transcendent. I wrestled with the immense enormity of such a principle for weeks, during my own private times of prayer and meditation. I found myself continually asking the Holy Spirit, inquiring of the LORD what could possibly be meant by such a powerful truth. It was difficult, also, to even begin to grapple with the feeling of personal responsibility such a Kingdom principle would represent. To the natural, religious mindset, the principle of Kingdom attraction comes as quite an inconvenient truth. Personal responsibility is always, to the natural mind, a very bitter pill. Yet, thankfully and prayerfully, as I began to receive the revelation of the universal Law of Attraction and as the Holy Spirit began to move within my own life, I became awakened not only to the immense power of my own thoughts but also to the power of my very own Identity. There is a reason, you see, that the name of my outreach around the globe is Identity Network. My identity, as well as yours, has always been that of Creator.

As darkness and nothingness – an empty vast sea of darkness – spanned what at the time could not even be defined as the cosmos, the mind of the Godhead existed perfectly. It was within this beautiful, creative mind that the images of all of Creation rested. Long before man ever enjoyed the garden paradise and long, long before a mate would ever be pulled from his side, the idea of marriage existed within the heart of GOD. Everything did. All things which now exist existed, first, within the Divine Mind of the Godhead. And then, in an instant, everything changed, as GOD spoke. As the

Spirit of GOD moved upon the vast and empty nothingness, all of existence began to come forth, springing forth into existence. It all began with a thought and with an inner vision. And so did the covenant of marriage. With His very own hand, the Creator fashioned what would be the hallmark of all Creation. That hallmark was man. And then came forth a female. Long before the Creator ever even considered reaching down into the dust of the earth below, though, the concept of the marriage relationship already existed within the Divine Mind of the Godhead. You and I existed there, also.

Long before the first argument took place – long before the term "spouse" was coined by human language and long, long before marriage began to feel so overwhelmingly difficult - there was only singularity and eternal oneness. There was no division. There was only a singular identity of perfection. Long before GOD ever spoke, though, GOD thought. As Creation manifested before our eyes and as we all looked on, the worlds were formed and stars were hurled into the vastness of what would come to be known as space. Then, there were no difficulties. There were no divorces. There was no guilt. Religion was not even a reality. How could it have been when there was no sense of separation from the Godhead? We were all so close. And there was such a great sense of togetherness. Though great diversity would emerge from the force of creative power, all things emerged from one, single source. That force was the light of GOD. And it lit up the worlds as He thought. I attempt, in rather futile fashion, to paint for you this picture so that you can try to imagine the eternal union and the eternal closeness form which we have all come – to which we will all return. And which we can all enjoy and experience now, the moment we become more awakened to the reality of the inner Kingdom of Heaven. Division and difficulty are matters of our own perspective. For every moment of chaos, there is the fact that it is all being worked together for our very own good. Is that not what the scriptures declare? That He, for His own pleasure and for the purpose of His own will is working all things together for our own good? So, knowing this, it's time to reconsider your definition of those things which can feel so, so very "difficult" at times. By doing this, though, you must also begin to reconsider the way in which you choose to view your own marriage connection with your spouse.

When I wrote my best-selling book *Attracting Your Godly Spouse*, I asked readers to begin to reassess all of their relationships in life and to begin to view the concept of relationship in a much, much more spiritual way

– from the perspective of the Law of Attraction at work within the Kingdom. I must admit that I've often been called "cynical" for my view that talk of finding "The One" can be quite an unhealthy venture. The truth, though, is that I'm a romantic at heart. I'm equally spiritual and practical, all at once. In the book, I asked that readers looking for love and hoping to find the love and romance of their dreams begin to become more active in finding their connections for true and lasting love. However, when speaking of the concept of marriage – the covenantal agreement of the divine union in the marriage bond – the term "One" truly does seem more fitting. Marriage is symbolic of the Oneness existing within the Godhead. When the LORD established the union of marriage, decreeing that two shall become one flesh, a picture of GOD was being painted for all of Creation to see. I've always found it very interesting and quite, quite remarkable, in fact, the idea that marriage literally came from within the individual who had been fashioned from the dust of the ground. In other words, the marriage union which Adam longed for existed within his own self the entire time. His partner – his help mate – was pulled forth from his own body, from deep within. From his literal side. What man needed as a help mate and partner existed, already on the inside of him. *"And the rib, which the Lord God had taken from man, made he a woman, and brought her unto the man. And Adam said, This is now bone of my bones, and flesh of my flesh: she shall be called Woman, because she was taken out of Man. Therefore shall a man leave his father and his mother, and shall cleave unto his wife: and they shall be one flesh." (Genesis 2:22-24 KJV)*

As you look to your spouse and see their actions or qualities and characteristics that can feel so troubling to you and seem so very difficult to deal with, there's a reason you're bothered as much as you are. That reason, quite simply put, is that you are being reminded of your own innate issues and of qualities and characteristics of your very own self which you despise. Marriage is, quite literally, a mirror by which you see yourself. In the very beginning of your love affair with your spouse, at the time in which there was instantaneous chemistry and a feeling of overwhelming attraction, you felt the magnetic drawing because you were seeing in your partner something that you felt within your very own self – hence the magnetism. Now, though, although it may seem as though the magnetism and chemistry is virtually nonexistent and replaced, instead, with anger and resentment, the reason you still feel as intensely as you do is because your spouse is mirroring the qualities which you yourself possess. There's a reason your partner is able to get underneath your skin and cause a rise of emotion within you and, remarkably enough, the reason has absolutely nothing to do with your spouse and literally everything to do with you. I'm sure right now you're probably thinking, "Jeremy, when are we going to focus on fixing my difficult spouse?" The answer to that question, my friend, rests in your own reflection when looking in the mirror. Since the union of marriage is a covenantal partnership and a reflection of your very own self, the way in which you will begin to bring healing into your marriage and, furthermore, healing to your difficult spouse is to begin to heal your very own self first. In a reflection, there exist identical parallels. The movement within one is mirrored and reflected within the other. If you truly desire to bring healing to your marriage, begin to look within your own life first.

In a May 2011 article for *Forbes* magazine, Carol Kinsey Goman detailed the science behind mirroring. In an article entitled "The Art and Science of Mirroring," Goman writes, *"The neuroscience behind limbic synchrony has everything to do with the discovery of mirror neurons and how empathy develops in the brain. In the late 1980s, researchers at the University of Parma in Italy found that the brain cells of macaque monkey fired in the same way whether they were making a particular motion (like reaching for a peanut) or watching another monkey or human make that movement. In terms of motor cell activity, the monkey's brain could not tell the difference between actually doing something and seeing it done. The scientists named those brain cells "mirror neurons." In human beings, it was found that mirror neurons not only simulate actions, they also reflect intentions and feelings. As such, they play a key role in our ability to socialize and empathize with others. Before the discovery of mirror neurons scientists generally believed that we used analytical thought processes to interpret and predict other people's motives and actions. Now, however, many have come to believe that we understand each other not by analysis, but through emotion. By reading body language signals (especially facial expressions) and automatically interpreting the emotion behind them, we get an intuitive sense of the world around us – without having to think about it."*

Mirroring is actually quite a spiritual and scientific thing. Scientific because at the core level it stems from or own neurological makeup and spiritual in that it involves emotion and feeling.

According to Goman, it is actually the innate desire to mirror emotions and feeling for the purpose of feeling a sense of closeness which triggers the outward actions of the mirroring effect. In other words, there actually is a very real scientific and spiritual reason as to why there can be such an intense, triggered emotion within you whenever your spouse does something that you find difficult or questionable. At the most basic and core level, it is because deep within a very real nerve is being struck – your own desire to be recognized. In those difficult moments, your soul is recognizing its very own self in another. There's an old saying which suggests than no one is capable of hurting us quite like those closest to us. There's truth in this statement, and anyone who has ever encountered heartbreak within a romantic relationship can attest to it. Those we love most can often times trigger within us the most pain and the most emotional turmoil. Not because they possess power over us but, rather, because we see in them something that we know we possess within our own selves. Within each relationship we encounter in life, particularly those of a more romantic or intimate nature, there exists a deeply rooted desire to relate and to connect at the deepest and most primal level. According to Goman, we as humans have an innate desire to see within another person the reflection of our own feelings and intentions. When difficult moments arise and when misunderstanding comes, the sense of security we seemed to have can become virtually nonexistent as we find ourselves wrestling with our own, inner onslaught of emotion.

Today, I want to encourage you to begin to recognize much more fully that you are not only an extension of your marriage but that you, in a very literal sense, are embodying the emotions of your spouse, as you are in covenantal agreement and divine alignment in the eyes of

Heaven. Now, though, having become awakened by the Holy Spirit to a far greater reality of union and oneness, why not begin to view even those difficult moments as simply teachable moments? Why not, rather than acting out in judgment and anger, begin to recognize that with each and every action of your spouse, the universe is asking you to look more deeply within your very own self. I assure you, my friend, the moment that you begin to become more consciously aware and spiritually awakened to the truth of Oneness, never again will you react from the place of judgement, with the desire to control. Rather, through the spirit of meekness and patience, you will begin to recognize that you, like your spouse, are a work in progress and that you are a part of a love story which is continually being written. You have been given grace. So show grace.

# DECLARATIONS OF LOVE

*"What you focus upon will continue to expand and to grow. So focus on gratefulness." – Jeremy Lopez*

In heated moments of strife, it can so often feel impossible to take a step back and to reassess. However, it's within the heated moments that a moment of reassessment is most crucial. Far too often, when difficulties arise within marriage, we give way to the chaotic and cathartic emotions of pain, anger, and resentment and, as a result, so often say things without giving very much conscious, focused thought. The entire time, though, because of the Law of Attraction within the Kingdom of Heaven, our words are still possessing creative and attractive power. There is no escaping the fact that in each and every moment, we are creating something. Our words are simply another catalyst through which emotion and intention are expressed and conveyed. In heated moments of strife and conflict, so much can become lost in translation, though. Although apologies can be given, words can never truly be taken back. They continue to linger and to resonate, still possessing the same power of the harnessed, focused intent with which they were first spoken. I often say that if you could see prophetically into the spiritual dimension even for a moment and actually recognize the very real and tangible power which accompanies spoken words, you would become much, much more careful when communicating and much more selective of the words you choose to use. Words possess the power of creation because they come from our own inner emotions and thoughts and are energetically laced with our own intention.

I've recently counseled a dear woman who had come to me seeking wisdom and a sense of direction in her marriage. She had recently married a man and although he seemed to be the answer to her every prayer, she found it was difficult to trust his love and affection for her because, like many of us, she still carried wounds from the past. Having survived a string of unsuccessful relationships which ended with painful breakups, when she came to Identity Network, she expressed to me how for years she had suffered the most excruciating emotional abuse imaginable. When I was a child, I heard some say, "Sticks and stones may break my ones but words will never hurt me." Well, it's just not true. It's a lie. In fact, in all honesty, often times the greatest abuse and the most lasting of damage come in the form of spoken words. Words that can never be taken back. Words which when spoken possess the power of creative, attractive force. With tears in her eyes, she said to me, "Jeremy, I'm not really sure how to be loved." Her words were painful to hear. They were genuine and authentic. She had gone through so much and in no way had deserved the pain she had been subjected to.

Although now married to the man of her dreams – a man who had been the literal answer to her prayers – she still found it difficult to trust. Above all, though, she found it difficult to let her guard down and become vulnerable. "I just don't really know how to let him in." She recognized the fact that her guardedness was unfair to him and even went as far as to say that he was the kindest and most patient man she had ever met before. Even when she found it difficult to believe, he continued to be patient and kind and affirming, always expressing his devotion to her and his love for her. The affirmations, though, seemed to fall upon deafened ears in the beginning of the marriage, though. Although she wanted to believe him when he confessed his love and devotion to her, she had heard far too many cutting, destructive words throughout her past. She had become scarred and emotionally damaged, and she recognized it. I share this with you, my friend, to say to you, quite simply, that words linger for a lifetime. Even when we are empowered and inspired by the Holy Spirit to become free, often, the process of integrating the wounds of the past can seem overwhelming. There is no way to take back the words we speak. The only choice we have is to simply recreate and to begin speaking new words. Where there were once only spoken words of death and judgement, we can begin to speak life and encouragement instead. Even then, though, the words of the past continue to linger, often haunting the recipient for years and years to come. This is never any more true than within the union of marriage, where the deepest levels of emotional and spiritual intimacy are concerned.

Anyone who claims that words have never hurt them are either lying or haven't lived long enough to be hurt. Words do hurt. Criticism cuts deeply. Since words are infused with the power of intention, the energy behind words and, more importantly, the way in which we interpret words, causes lasting impressions and ripple effects for generations. The scriptures declare that even the power of blessing and cursing lies within the words we speak. *"Out of the same mouth proceedeth blessing and cursing. My brethren, these things ought not so to be." (James 3:10 KJV)* Whether you realize it or not, there have been moments in which you've cursed your marriage and cursed your spouse with the words you've spoken. It's all too common, really, and these curses can often come in even the most subtle of ways. "He can be so lazy." "She spends entirely way too much money." "He's never home" "She never cooks." Although often said in jest, the words continue to linger, and the universe recognizes them as declarations of your own creative, attractive power. With our words, you and I are constantly making declarations throughout the day – even when we fail to realize it. From the time we awaken in the morning to the time we rest at night and even while we are sleeping, the mind and the emotions are continually pronouncing these declarations over our lives and over all aspects of our marriage. The moment, though, that we place articulation and verbalization to these thoughts and intentions, something even more remarkable begins to happen. The thoughts and the emotions become much more harnessed – more powerful.

When the Holy Spirit first began to awaken me all those years ago to the immense power we possess within our thoughts, He also showed me that such creative power is only amplified when harnessed through our words. Jesus, when teaching the divine and heavenly principles of the Kingdom even said as much. *"For verily I say unto you, That whosoever shall say unto this mountain, Be thou removed, and be thou cast into the sea; and shall not doubt in his heart, but shall believe that those things which he saith shall come to pass; he shall have whatsoever he saith." (Mark 11:23 KJV)* I choose to believe that Jesus meant what he said. The teaching wasn't merely an allegory or some analogy. Rather, it was a testament to the creative element residing within spoken words. In other words, quite literally, you shall have *whatsoever* you say.   Right now, as you look to your marriage and to the feeling of difficulty and disconnectedness, you are being given a choice to either bless or to curse and, if you were to be completely honest with yourself, you would admit that in times past, many of the curses have come forth from your very own lips.   Right now, in this moment, as difficult as it might seem to grapple with such transcendent truth and as painful as it might be to come to terms with the role that you've, at times, played within your own destructive force, the reality is that you are now experiencing everything you have spoken.

You are seeing the words of yesterday and yesteryear in full manifestation before your very eyes.   If he being difficult?   We'll, you've affirmed as much in heated moments of disagreement.   Does he fail to listen?   Well, you've constantly told him as much.   Does she not communicate well? You've constantly criticized her for it, and she's doing exactly what you've affirmed to her. Does he never seem to want to spend time with you anymore? Well, you've contributed to that for years with the words you've spoken. The Biblical Law of Attraction is quite an inconvenient truth because it reminds us of the role that we play within our own creation. Words are catalysts through which our intention and creative power are conveyed to the universe.

It was within my own personal life and in business all those years ago that I was forced to confront the power of words. As the Holy Spirit awakened me to the truth of the creative force lying within me, I began to become much, much more conscious of the words I spoke. In those early days, there were no publishing contracts, there were no books, and there was no worldwide ministry. As I've shared within my books, it wasn't until I began to take responsibility for my thoughts, my own inner vision and, also, my own words, that success began to come to me. I attracted into my life the vision I wanted. By becoming more keenly aware of the power of my own words, success began to literally overtake me. Success tracked me down even in my dreams, it seemed. I began to speak blessings over my life and ministry. In those early days, at the turn of the millennium, few people were talking about the power of attraction; however, in spite of criticism and confrontation, I continued to speak blessings over my life. When criticisms came, I spoke blessings over myself and encouraged myself in the LORD instead. Then, the phone began to ring. Publishers began to reach out to me to offer book deals. I began to be booked at conferences. In only a matter of months, the ministry of Identity Network reached a global, worldwide audience. To this day, though, I still remain cognizant and ever-vigilant of my own words and thoughts, careful always to remember that the same creative and attractive power of the Kingdom which brings success must be utilized in order to keep and to maintain that success. The same, though, can and must be said of your marriage. The same creative and attractive power which first kindled the love affair with your spouse is the exact same creative and attractive power which must be remembered and recognized if you are going to rekindle your intimacy once again and bring forth restoration and healing into your marriage bond.

It's time to not only become more of a blessing to your spouse but it's time to actually pronounce blessing. Often times, without ever even realizing it, the first step toward becoming a blessing is to begin to be more conscious of the words we speak. Today, I'm giving you an assignment. I want you to begin to pronounce blessings rather than curses, as difficult as such a task might seem within the heated moments of disagreement. Even when it's difficult and even when the feeling of anger and resentment is present, I want you to begin to make a conscious choice to use your words much more wisely. In heated moments of disagreement, if you feel the sense of anger and resentment, make a conscious choice to affirm the *opposite* of that feeling. When your spouse does something that literally pushes you toward your breaking point, take a moment, reassess and recalibrate, and affirm the opposite of that feeling. Both on the conscious and subconscious level, by doing this, you are reprogramming your own energy and reforming the neural pathways within your brain to exemplify a better and more wholesome feeling than that of anger and resentment. This is due, in part, to the science of neuroplasticity and has even more to do with the creative power of the Law of Attraction. With each feeling comes a very real choice. You are being given a front row seat, in each moment, and a divine opportunity to actually look behind your thoughts and feelings. I would encourage you to make the right choice in what you choose to verbalize and articulate.

Emotions exist in a very spiritual way, as sort of the inner gauge of the soul. What you feel and what you think says much, much more about you than it does about your spouse. Remember, you are responsible for your own reactions and only you can be responsible for responding in a more loving and blessed way. Am I negating or attempting to dismiss the fact that, yes, there are feelings that will literally seem to cut you to your core? Absolutely not. What I am saying, though, is that just because you feel the anger and the resentment in those very difficult moments doesn't mean that you have to give them place and it most certainly does not mean that you have to bring them into the physical, natural world by affirming them. Think of each word as a form through which intention is brought forth into the natural, physical world. Do feeling and emotion exist without words? Absolutely. However, by verbalizing the emotion you are literally encapsulating it and sending it out into the universe in a much more forceful, harnessed way. Mindful communication takes practice, I'll admit; however, as with all things, change has to begin somewhere. It may as well start with you.

As you study the scriptures, you will find that not only did Jesus teach that creative power lies within words but that, also, throughout the entirety of scripture the principle of mindful communication is shared repeatedly. Allow me to share with you a few examples of this. Proverbs 11:9 declares, *"Evil words destroy one's friends; wise discernment rescues the godly."* Proverbs 11:12 says, *"It is foolish to belittle a neighbor; a person with good sense remains silent."* Proverbs 11:17 says, *"Your own soul is nourished when you are kind, but you destroy yourself when you are cruel."* Proverbs 15:1 states, *"A gentle answer turns away wrath, but hard words stir up anger."* Proverbs 15:4 says, *"Gentle words bring life and health; a deceitful tongue crushes the spirit."* Proverbs 16:24 states, *"Kind words are like honey–sweet to the soul and healthy for the body."* And Proverbs 18:4 declares, *"A person's words can be life-giving water; words of true wisdom are as refreshing as a bubbling brook."* As you can see, words and the emotions we articulate truly possess the power to change atmospheres. Words build up and edify or they tear down and destroy, but they are always, always creating something and bringing into manifestation within the physical, three-dimensional world *exactly* what they are intended to do.

It's time to begin declaring love and gratefulness over your spouse again, as difficult as it might seem. Perhaps, as you read these words, you and your spouse have argued so much that to actually begin to encourage him or her would seem like quite a challenge. Maybe you've fought so hard that anger now seems much like second nature. However, anger is not your nature. Resentment is not who you truly are. You can recreate and begin to build again, rather than tearing down and eroding the foundation of your home and your marriage bond. You may ask, "Well, Jeremy, where do I even begin to do this?" Start by focusing on the good rather than the bad. Sure, there may be moments of difficulty which literally feel as though they're driving you toward your breaking point. And yes, chances are he does anger you in some way. But there are good qualities there as well. Is he a good provider? Then affirm that. Is he a hard worker? Affirm that. Does she care for the children and is she a good mother? Begin your change by affirming that.

I promise you, my friend, you'll be surprised to find just how far a little more kindness will go once you begin to recognize the power you truly possess within you. And when you say it, mean it. Allow yourself to feel it. Become more thoughtful with the emotion and the feeling behind the words. Take a moment before affirming and recognize just how hard your husband or wife works. Attempt to place yourself within their shoes. When your husband returns from work, rather than meeting him with criticism and harsh judgment over what he hasn't done, affirm, instead, what he has done and highlight his accomplishments. Maybe he hasn't taken the trash out yet or completed the repair; however, he has worked to provide for the family hasn't he? Perhaps she hasn't prepared dinner, but she has taken the kids to soccer practice, attended the parent-teacher meeting, and cleaned. In today's society, I feel women deserve so much credit. No one works harder than a loving mother. It's time to give your wife the credit she deserves and begin to affirm all of her amazing qualities. The same is said for a hard working husband.

When you begin to recognize the power of your own words, you will never again throw stones in the same way. You begin to change your marriage by changing the atmosphere of your marriage. This begins by becoming more consciously aware and more mindful of the things you say. It's time to begin to practice mindful communication if you truly do wish to see a change within your marriage and a change within your spouse. Far too often, you've allowed yourself to be a victim to your own emotions and your own feelings. This is not the truth, though. The truth of the matter is that you, by divine design, are fully aware, fully capable, and fully in control of your responses and your reactions, in spite of the emotion or the feelings which can at times seem so overwhelming. Today, in closing this chapter, I want to encourage you, if you truly have a heartfelt desire to bring healing to your marriage once again, begin to make declarations of love rather than declarations of destruction. The moment you begin to see and recognize that you have been a contributing factor to the turmoil, the chaos, and the difficulty you are now experiencing because of your words, you will begin to become more mindful in your communication and will begin to bless rather than curse. Remember, what you affirm, you will continue to manifest within your marriage. Why not begin to embody the change you wish to see? Healing begins with a decision to become more mindful.

# THE HIGHER TRUTHS

*"There's a big difference between going to church and being the church." – Jeremy Lopez*

As I began writing this book and as the Holy Spirit began speaking to me concerning the topic of dealing with "difficult" spouses, I realized the need to include this chapter that I'm entitling "The Higher Truths." Here at the offset, as we begin this chapter, I'll admit, in total transparency that you may not feel very comfortable as you read this. In fact, chances are there will be a moment within this chapter when I will strike a nerve; however, I promise you, this chapter is needed. I assure, you, also, that you'll be fine and if you can process this truth and receive it into your spirit you will begin to see a drastic and remarkable change within your marriage like never before. As the Holy Spirit was speaking to me regarding this chapter, I must admit, I found myself asking, "LORD, are you sure you want me to say that? If so, then how?" I know beyond the shadow of a doubt, though, that this is perhaps one of the most important chapters within this book, and my humble and heartfelt prayer is that these words will pierce your heart and get down deeply into your spirit to plant the seeds of change. So, there. Now that the disclaimer is out of the way, allow me to say that chances are you're being far, far too religious within your marriage relationship. There. I said it. It needed to be said.

In moments of coaching married couples who come to Identity Network, one thing that I hear time and time and time again, without fail, is, "Jeremy, I keep praying and praying for my husband, but no matter what, my husband never wants to go to church with me." If I were to be completely honest and transparent with you, this issue is perhaps the issue that I hear more than all other issues. More than issues of trust, issues of intimacy, and issues of finance is the issue of a spouse not wanting to attend church. If this applies to you, then I understand your frustration. I promise you that I do. However, although I love and admire your faithfulness, the truth of the matter is that you're actually hurting your spouse rather than helping him or her by continuing to push the issue. Of that, I assure you. The issue is all too common though and I promise you that you aren't alone in your struggle. Within the union of marriage, there exists an innate need and desire to connect spiritually with our partners. Although this is a very real need and I never want to casually dismiss your desire, I must say that, more times than not, this desire actually stems from a critical and religious Pharisee spirit rather than a true desire to share a spiritual intimacy with your spouse. I know that may strike a nerve deeply within you, but it's the truth. The reason the Holy Spirit asked that I include this chapter to you within the book is because He wants you to begin to reassess your true and genuine motives. As I shared earlier, the passage of scripture concerning being "equally yoked" has absolutely nothing at all to do with what we would consider "Christianity." Again, I say this with all love and with all grace.

At the beginning of the book, I made a remark that you may have found rather questionable, and within this chapter I'm going to elaborate. I've phrased the questionable comment intentionally in order to spark within you a curiosity which, my prayer is, will lead you to passionately pursue the discovery of your own, hidden motives. Earlier, I said that it doesn't matter to me if my doctor or my lawyer or my co-workers are professing "Christians" and that my genuine concern is that they are competent and fit and qualified to do the work that I hire them to do. I stand by that statement entirely. If you know me then you know, firsthand, that nothing – absolutely nothing – is more important to me than spreading the Gospel of Jesus Christ around the globe, and for more than twenty years that has been the heart, soul and driving force behind the work and global outreach of Identity Network and my own ministry ventures throughout the years. However, where the issue of your marriage is concerned, if you truly desire to bring healing and wholeness and love and acceptance into your marriage and into your home, you're going to have to stop bringing the issue of "Evangelization" into your marriage in an attempt to force your beliefs upon your spouse.

If he or she doesn't share your beliefs identically or if they question your beliefs, I promise you, my friend, it's alright, GOD is still sovereign, it isn't the end of the world, and, hear me, it doesn't have to be the end of your marriage. If you are considering leaving and walking out of your marriage because your husband or wife doesn't profess to be "Christian" or if he or she chooses to not go to church with you, my friend, that is arrogance, ignorance, and downright stupidity. And it will be a decision that will haunt you for the rest of your life, I promise. I say that with all love and with all grace. But, it does need to be said.

These are issues that should have been addressed long before the marriage covenant was ever even entered into. But, perhaps you've come to Christ years into your marriage. So, now what? What does that mean for you? Are you to continue to witness and to evangelize your marriage by constantly bombarding your spouse with your own beliefs, preconceived notions, and sense of right and wrong? Absolutely not, and, although it isn't very popular to say, particularly in our overtly religious culture, the scriptures do make this principle quite clear and there is no escaping it. If this is striking a nerve within you, well, chances are it's because you're being controlled by a religious, Jezebel spirit. Control and manipulation disguising itself as "Christianity" is not the Holy Spirit. You don't need deliverance, though, my friend. You simply need a fresh perspective. And *that* is the reason for this chapter within this book. It's time to begin to reassess your own, hidden motives and intentions. It's time to take a long, hard look in the mirror and begin to see that the Holy Spirit is still in full operation within your marriage, even when it may not seem like it outwardly.

Above all, it's high time you begin to reassess your definition of "Christianity."

I'm about to make a very controversial statement, so fair warning. But if your pastor, a so-called prophet, or anyone else claiming to be in a position of spiritual authority ever suggests to you that you should consider leaving your marriage because your husband isn't going to church with you, then then that man or woman is a liar, a charlatan, a con-artist, and nothing more than a fraud and false prophet. Yes, you read that correctly. My friend, if love truly does bear all things and hope for all things, as the Apostle Paul clearly states, then the issue of whether or not your spouse goes to church with you is, truly, a non-issue. Again, it's time we begin to reassess our definition of "Christianity." So often, particularly within our overtly religious society – particularly here in the west – we forget that Jesus and the apostles never carried Bibles and, at the time the gospels and epistles were recorded, the idea of "church" looked quite different than it does today in our more modern culture. That isn't to say that church isn't important and that isn't to insinuate that the "ecclesia," the "Body," doesn't serve some very real and powerful purpose within the world today. What it does mean, though, is that, at the end of the day, GOD is far, far less concerned with what happens inside your church building on Sunday mornings and much, much more concerned with whether or not you are exhibiting the love of GOD within your own personal marriage and to the rest of the world.

I'll never forget a client named Patricia who had come to me for insight regarding the issue of her marriage. For years she had prayed for her husband to find Christ and profess Christianity as his religion. More than anything, it seemed, Patricia wanted her husband to attend church with her.  I admired her zeal and her faith.  However, as we talked and as she shared, Patricia revealed to me how on more than one occasion she felt the LORD leading her to leave the marriage because her husband, Mike, simply refused to go.  Now, on the surface level, at first glance, it may have seemed that her desires were authentic and pure – that she simply wanted her husband to share in her faith.  However, upon further examination, it quickly became quite, quite obvious to me, through the discernment of the Holy Spirit, that Patricia's true intention actually had nothing at all to do with Christ and, instead, had everything to do with her own desire to control and to manipulate her husband.  I told her, as the Word of the LORD came to me, that if she left her marriage over such an issue that she would regret the decision and be haunted for the rest of her life.  She didn't listen.  Instead, taking the advice of other so-called prophets and even the advice of her own pastor, she filed for divorce shortly after our encounter and is now in another marriage. Ironically, though, her second marriage is far more tumultuous and recently I received a request from Patricia for a prophetic word in which she says she's considering filing for divorce again because her husband hasn't, as she puts it, been "Baptized in the Holy Spirit."

Now, I in no way share that very real example as a way to dismiss Patricia's feeling, and I in no way seek to suggest that there isn't a need to be led by the power of the Holy Spirit. What I am saying, though, is that Patricia's faith in no way served as the basis of her decision, regardless of what she claimed, because her actions proved otherwise. You see, this is why I said earlier that someone professing to be "Christian" or going to church means very little to me. Show me actions. Although I in no way doubt Patricia's love of the LORD, I do sincerely doubt her love for people. Her motives revealed themselves. I continue to pray for her daily, hoping that she will finally find the peace she so desperately deserves and needs. Religion, you see, is nothing more than just a vicious cycle of repetition, fueled by the ego and by one's desire to control others. That's all religion truly is, really. Nothing more than that. Sure, we turn a blinded eye because we love the LORD and claim that our religion is the ultimate, higher truth – better than everyone else's – but, at the end of the day, "Christianity," by definition is really nothing more than just another world religion. Just another social club claiming to have all the answers. So yes, my friend, I'm far, far less concerned with the term "Christian" and much, much more concerned with the truth of the Holy Spirit and the nature of "Christ." Terms and labels and definitions mean absolutely nothing to me. Love matters. Faithfulness to giving matters. Compassion matters. And, where your marriage is concerned, yes, patience and longsuffering matter.

When I was completing my doctoral dissertation all those years ago, studying the historical beginnings of the early church, I was shocked to find that the church at Jerusalem in very few ways resembled the churches we see today. There were no Bibles, because those wouldn't come about until centuries later. There were no Christian church buildings as we now recognize them. There were no "sermons" preached, as we would, today, recognize them. No. Instead, there were only families – mothers and fathers and sisters and brothers – all coming together within homes to think of the reality of Christ. In fact, according to the scriptures, the apostles actually weren't even called

"Christians" until the missionary journey into Antioch and, even then, it was used as a derogatory term. The apostles never professed to be "Christian." They never needed to. They were aware of Christ and they loved people and, as a result, the miracles confirmed their words to be truth. Today, though, centuries and centuries later, we would rather judge others over the usage of words and terms and labels, criticizing them for not believing like us and saying that simply because they do not share our beliefs identically that they somehow are wrong or faithless. I have a dear friend who, like so, so many, left the church years ago. When he did, many said to him, "Well, it's obvious you don't even believe in GOD any longer." He responded, simply, "I do believe in GOD. I just can no longer agree with all of you."

You see, my friend, we must get over this idea that we have some sort of copyright on the

Holy Spirit. The Holy Spirit is truly moving within the lives of all men and women at all times – even those who do not share in our beliefs.

When we think of marriage, we think of union and partnership. Surprisingly, Jesus viewed the importance of marriage in a much different way than we seem to today in our modern culture. *"And it came to pass, that when Jesus had finished these sayings, he departed from Galilee, and came into the coasts of Judaea beyond Jordan; And great multitudes followed him; and he healed them there. The Pharisees also came unto him, tempting him, and saying unto him, Is it lawful for a man to put away his wife for every cause? And he answered and said unto them, Have ye not read, that he which made them at the beginning made them male and female, And said, For this cause shall a man leave father and mother, and shall cleave to his wife: and they twain shall be one flesh? Wherefore they are no more twain, but one flesh. What therefore God hath joined together, let not man put asunder. They say unto him, Why did Moses then command to give a writing of divorcement, and to put her away? He saith unto them, Moses because of the hardness of your hearts suffered you to put away your wives: but from the beginning it was not so. And I say unto you, Whosoever shall put away his wife, except it be for fornication, and shall marry another, committeth adultery: and whoso marrieth her which is put away doth commit adultery." (Matthew 19:1-9 KJV)* I fail to see how having a spouse who doesn't want to go to church with you constitutes grounds for divorce – or even "difficulty" for that matter.

My friend, do you truly desire your spouse to begin attending church with you and profess Christ? If so, then stop asking. Stop asking, stop quoting scriptures, stop evangelizing to them, and stop mentioning the need and the importance for church. The greatest tools for evangelization are love and acceptance and patience and an understanding of people. Have you considered that perhaps the single greatest reason your spouse wants nothing to do with your faith is because you haven't fully been putting your own faith into practice within the confines of your own marriage? Have you considered that maybe, just maybe, the issue isn't a lack of faith on the part of your spouse but, rather, is a mixed message and inconsistency on your part? You can't profess the need for Christ and remain unloving and critical. You can't say to your spouse that he or she needs to attend church with you and then condemn them for not sharing in your beliefs. I mean, let's face it. Is it any wonder, really, why your faith doesn't seem very attractive to him or her? Is it any wonder, really, why your spouse continues to say that your Christianity is hypocrisy? If you truly want to see the transformative power of Christ within your marriage, stop preaching and start loving. Stop quoting scriptures and anointing the walls of your home with oil and begin, instead, to anoint your spouse with words and actions of understanding, compassion, and patience. By entering into the agreement of marriage, you have entered into the oldest institution ever designed and established by GOD – older than even that of the Christian church.

Long before there was ever the mandate to spread the gospel to the uttermost parts of the earth, there was a man and a woman. Long before the missionary journeys ever began, there was love. Centuries before Jesus ever climbed atop the hill to become the sacrificial atonement for the sins of the world, there was marriage.

Stop losing sight of that because of your own religious indoctrination. I promise you, if your spouse doesn't attend church with you, it isn't the end of the world and it should never become the end of your marriage. You are most faithful to GOD when you are faithful to love. Always remember                                        that.

# THE CALL TO CREATE

*"Stop blaming the devil and start taking responsibility for your own creation." – Jeremy Lopez*

As a prophetic minister, a counselor, and a prophetic life coach, my responsibility is to always be real and transparent with you. Many times, throughout more than twenty years of the work and the outreach of ministry, I've often heard, "Jeremy, I can't believe you said that." Well, what I've found throughout years of ministry is that the world doesn't need more religious platitudes or more religious clichés. The world and humanity need a dose of reality, and I strive to be as real with you as I possibly can. Authenticity is a foundational key to a successful marriage. Miracles of transformation and healing begin to spontaneously take place when we begin to become more authentic and more transparent within our own selves. In order for the miracle of healing to take place, though, first, there are masks that must be removed and true and authentic reflections that must be recognized. My friend, I want to encourage you to become more authentic within your bond of marriage. I want you, today, to remove the mask.

As one with a prophetic gifting, my responsibility is to declare the Word of the LORD to the nations of the earth. As a life coach, my responsibility is to encourage, to build up, and to edify by sharing universal principles and strategies. However, as a follower of Christ, my responsibility is to walk in truth and transparency in all areas of life, and the truth of the matter is that we can only begin to become more authentic and transparently real and present the moment we take off the masks we've been hiding behind. Is it frightening? Yes. Is it often difficult? Yes. However, I assure you, my friend, there is absolutely nothing more difficult or draining than living a life that is a lie. Of that, I can assure you. A factor which is contributing to the difficulty within your marriage is that you haven't fully begun to understand you own personality. How can you truly accept, honor, and understand the personality of another person when you yourself haven't fully recognized who you truly are? It's all too common, really. Almost daily, I encounter young, beautiful couples whose bonds of romance and chemistry are fueled with passion and desire. Young couples who, when first meeting, are filled with dreams and desires and an optimism regarding the future. Then engagements happen. Then comes marriage. And somewhere along the way, the passion begins to die and the chemistry seems to become nonexistent. In other words what seemed to once exist so plainly in the beginning begins to seem so lost and long gone.

As radical an idea as it might seem, though, I'd like to propose to you that the amazing spark of chemistry has never really gone away or has died, as much as it is that it's simply been covered up. It's been "masked." In the beginning, when boy meets girl – or when anyone meets anyone else, really – there exists the strange, otherworldly, and often times overwhelming spark of magnetism. I discuss much more of the spiritual mechanics behind attraction in my book *Attracting Your Godly Spouse*; however, for now, suffice it to say that in romantic connections there is always a very real spiritual element existing at the core, behind the scenes and just outside of natural sight. This chemistry can be felt physically, though, and there's a reason for it. That reason being that the soul is always authentic. You, as a divine, spiritual being are not your body but are, rather, the soul existing within the body. As I've shared and taught for years, you and I aren't physical beings here to try to find a spiritual experience. Rather, we are spiritual beings here to enjoy and to learn from the human experience. Recognizing this removes the sense of condemnation once and for all. You're a human being for a reason, so you may as well learn to enjoy it. One of the most enjoyable and pleasurable aspects of the human experience is the element of connection and relationship. By divine design, you and I have been created to experience relationships in all their many, varying forms. Some relationships are platonic, while others are much more intimate. Above them all, though, towering head and shoulders above the rest, is the institution of the marriage bond – a sacred union blessed and ordained within the corridors of Heaven.

When a connection is made – particularly those of a more romantic nature – behind the overwhelming sense of magnetism and the emotions commonly associated with the feeling of chemistry, lies an innate desire to relate. After all, isn't that the basis of all of our relationships? Two individuals seeking to relate to each other?  In the beginning of your marriage, there was such a sense of being able to relate. Chances are, during your engagement, during those late night calls which lasted for hours, you and your partner were probably even able to finish each other's sentences. There was a commonality. It seemed that the two of you were inseparable and joined spiritually even then – long before ever even exchanging marriage vows. Somewhere, along the way, though, all of those feelings have become lost in translation and the spark of chemistry and the feeling of desire have been replaced with emotions of anger, resentment, and, quite possibly, even the feelings of hatred and disgust. So, what happened? I mean, what *exactly* happened?

Was it that you simply grew out of love? Was it that you simply began to change your mind? Or was it something else entirely? Was it, rather, that you weren't even truly yourself in the beginning? As shocking as it might seem, what if I were to suggest to you that the difficulties you now experience within your marriage are not the result of a difficult spouse and they haven't arisen simply because you've suddenly and miraculously had a change of heart – even though it may seem that way on the outside and feel that way to you emotionally. What if I were to tell you that you've simply begun to finally be yourself at last and that the difficulty is arising because for a long, long time you've been wearing a mask to cover your own personality? Marriage has a way of forcing us to remove our masks. What if the issue truly isn't your difficult spouse as much as it is, since entering into the marriage covenant, you've simply become so comfortable that you've removed a mask that you'd been wearing the entire time? Allow me to explain.

In my recent book *Attracting Your Godly Spouse*, I shared how, quite often, when relationships first begin, there is almost always a desire to mask our true selves. This can often stem from our own insecurities and from our own fear of vulnerability; however, more times than not, it arises from the desire to impress. I'm sure you're familiar with what I mean by this. Whether because of a desire to impress or because of a desire to simply hide behind our own walls, we all wear masks at times.

However, in the beginning stages of a relationship, these masks are all too prevalent. "I'll pretend to like his taste in music." "I'll exaggerate my income when she asks." "I'll casually omit the fact that I filed for bankruptcy. She'll never know." "I'll let him think having children really isn't that big of a deal to me." "I'll tell her I completed my master's degree." All of these masks, though seemingly innocent and harmless when a relationship first begins to develop, over time, as the relationship grows, become cancers which erode the foundation of the marriage union. Before you know it, two years have passed, or four, or ten, and in the blink of an eye the issues that once seemed at the time to be so minor and so insignificant begin to resurface with a vengeance. What was once "I really enjoy that band" has become, "Why can't I trust you?" What, in a night of passion, was once, "I work in management" has become "Why isn't there ever enough money?" You see, although we all at times wear these masks, masks are always, always forcefully removed when the marriage vows are exchanged and when reality begins to set in. Again, the universe always, always demands authenticity and transparency and so it's best to go into the connection with authenticity to begin with.

Now, though, as you find yourself reeling with emotion and grappling with a taste of betrayal and distrust, questing whether or not you ever truly did know your spouse, the universe is asking you to look more deeply within the story of your own life as well. Were there moments when you hid behind your own façade and built walls of distancing as a way to protect yourself? If you were to be completely honest with yourself, the answer might be painful and uncomfortable to admit. Deep down, you know the answer to that question. Often times, it can seem rather shocking the "issues" that seem to suddenly surface out of the blue and randomly within a marriage. If you begin to look more closely, though, the issues and the difficult moments truly aren't as random and as unexpected as they might sometimes seem. They all had a beginning moment. They all began with a small, subtle intention of deceit. Every issue within your marriage began, first, as a mask. Yes. Even the most major of disagreements began, first, with a desire to hide. There is no escaping this simple yet all-powerful principle of the Kingdom of Heaven within. The universe, because of the power of creation, has consistently and perfectly given you exactly what you once said you wanted. This is another reason, my friend, why it is so vitally important to not only be conscientious and more mindful of our communication but also much more in touch with our own personalities.

When we think of the idea of personality, our minds often drift toward the outward. We think of qualities and characteristics exhibited by a person. However, spiritually speaking, the truth of the matter is that in order to truly understand the mechanics behind the formation and development of one's own personality, we must begin to reassess the definition of the word "person." The term is derived from the Latin "persona" which, interestingly enough, was originally a term used to depict the many different "roles" a character would play within a theatrical performance. In ancient times, it was not uncommon for a single actor to embody multiple roles within a play, often wearing various different masks to help define each "role." Knowing this, now, let's take a closer look at the personality you now find yourself bringing into your own marriage and your own love union. In truth, you probably now find yourself wearing many different hats, so to speak. You're a wife or a husband. You're a business professional. You're a mother or a father, perhaps. You are a son or daughter. You have friendship connections. All various, different roles. Yet, beneath it all, at the core level, there is the real you – the true and authentic you. The you that feels emotion so deeply and who, at times, becomes overwhelmed. The real you – the soul you – is a complex amalgamation of the mind, the will, and the emotion and you are constantly, day in and day out, being forced to process what you think, what you want, and what you feel, In the chaos of it all, though, so much can often times become lost in translation and the need to become much, much more authentic and transparent can, at times, begin to feel like more of a juggling act than a lesson in spirituality and self-awareness.

If you truly and genuinely want to bring a sense of wholeness and healing into your marriage union, you're going to have to remove the mask. Even more importantly, though, you're also going to have to begin to assess the root cause of why it is that you've felt you've needed to wear a mask to begin with. Only you can find the answer to that, friend. My job, prophetically speaking, is simply to encourage you to begin to look deeper and to begin to come from a much more authentic place. Right now, as you read these words, chances are you find yourself living within a marriage that has become unsatisfying to you. It's alright to admit that. What's not alright, though, is to blame your spouse for the very things that you've been guilty of. It's unfair. It's wrong. The behavior is cancerous and is eroding away the foundation the pair of you have been attempting to build. What's also not fair to your marriage or to your spouse is to say that you haven't in some way contributed to the issues at hand. In order to fully recognize this, though, requires a little more thoughtfulness and the often difficult work of personal introspection. I want you to look back. Back before the kids, before the career, and before it all seemed so, so very difficult. Look back to when it first began. Who were you? Who were you wanting to become? I ask these questions because perhaps they will in some small way help you to better and more accurately discern what were your true motives and intentions during those formative moments of the relationship. I'm in no way seeking to suggest that your entire marriage has been built upon lies and deception. But what I am saying, though, is that in order to heal your marriage and bring wholeness again, you're going to have to begin to be honest – honest with yourself and honest about your true motives.

It is only in moments of brutal, often painful honesty that the work of healing can truly begin. And the universe is demanding that of you. All of Heaven and earth, because of the power of attraction, is giving you exactly what you've said you wanted. And now, all these years later, you're experiencing it each and every day within your marriage. The brutally honest truth of the matter, my friend, is that you can't go back. You aren't supposed to. However, you can begin to recreate. You do this by beginning to think new thoughts and to begin to harness a brand new intention. Today, you're given the chance to begin to create all over again and to start afresh and anew. This time, though, be honest with yourself, finally.

# THE POWER OF MEMORY

*"You and your spouse are constantly creating memories.   Make them good." –
Jeremy Lopez*

I want to take you upon a journey.  As we,
together, embark upon this journey, I want you
to become keenly aware of the sights and
sounds – the scenery – as we move forward.  I
want you to also begin to allow yourself to feel
the many, many emotions that arise within you
as you notice the changing scenery.  Today, as
we embark upon this journey, we are not only
looking back to a time when things were much,
much simpler, but we are looking back to a time
when the love and chemistry within your love
affair was palpable.  Others used to take notice.
When you brought him home to meet your

family for the very first time, you were different. You could hardly contain the joy and the overwhelming love as he sat beside you at the family dinner table and as your father created all those awkward moments when they asked him all of those questions about himself. In truth, you were so uncomfortable that you wanted to run and hide. You held his hand as he answered. There were so, so many amazing and remarkable moments then. Not only did you adore him, but your family began to adore him as well. They had never seen you so very happy before. When you looked at him, you could see the rest of your life. And you welcomed it. You were, both, so young, so exuberant – so free. You had always prayed for a man like him, and, to your astonishment and your amazement, you found that such a man did exist and that, even more remarkably, he wanted to be all yours. The chemistry and the desire were overwhelming in those days. The two of you could hardly wait until your weeding day to express your love to each other physically. Maybe you didn't wait, in fact. At the time, it seemed like waiting would be an impossible task. For the two of you, maybe it was. The love was intense. It was fiery and spiritual. When you first became intimate, it seemed as though you had found your very own soul perfectly embodied and encapsulated within the body of another human being. It was miraculous.

When he asked you to marry him, you couldn't contain the excitement. You both wept tears of joy and happiness. You did that "ugly cry" that you've always been so very self-conscious about. When your wedding day came, the day was as magical as one could possibly hope for. It was the stuff of fairy tales and dreams. You both looked radiant and the joy was electric. Everyone in attendance could feel it as the air was charged with joy and longing. A prayer had been answered, it seemed. The honeymoon was equally as magical, as the two of you embarked upon what would be the rest of your lives. So many, many memories were made there. Before long, the children began to arrive. In the beginning they only added to the immense feeling of joy. They, too, were answers to prayers prayed long ago. Time began to pass. Birthdays and holidays were celebrated, as all holidays and birthdays go. There were times of exceedingly great joy. There was also loss, at times. Through it all, though, there was a sense of togetherness and a bond of unshakable familiarity. You and your spouse were in love and, in spite of whatever would come, you at least knew that the two of you were in it together, prepared to take on the entire world if need be. Above all, though, you felt safe. And the feeling of safety was matched only by the feeling of life. Every day was an adventure.

Somewhere along the way, though, you both became increasingly forgetful. It suddenly became difficult to even remember what had once, at times before, seemed so very magical. A senses of euphoria and nostalgia become replaced with a feeling of amnesia, as, together, you both began to wonder what had suddenly begun to seem so very lost. I wanted to include this chapter for you, as a way to remind you of the way things were. In the beginning – long before things ever began to feel so overwhelmingly difficult. There were promises made then. Promises which, in truth, came from very authentic emotions and very real feelings and very pure intentions. Time – the ever-elusive element – has a way of causing us to become increasingly more forgetful, though, as the journey of life continues. Today, as you read these words, the love affair that once seemed to be the stuff of legends has become the things of nightmares for you. Each day, rather than being a joyous adventure, has become an overwhelming burden – difficult to survive and even more difficult to manage successfully. Now, the slightest stresses seem to become bombs detonated deep within. You try to hold your tongue and not complain, but deep within you have an innate sense of dissatisfaction and discontentedness. It's alright to admit that. As time has passed, old wounds have surfaced over and over again. And now, as you find yourself reading these words, it seems as though the time in the beginning – the time when love was real – was nothing more than a dream. Did it ever even really exist? Was there ever really a true and lasting love there to begin with?

The answer, my friend, is a resounding yes. Love was there. Love did exist. And, in spite of the calamity and the noise of the war which now rages within you, driving more deeply between you and your spouse the wedge of resentment, believe it or not, it still exists. It's still there. It's still as strong. Although, admittedly, it's a little more difficult to feel. I'm writing this chapter to you as an encouragement to begin to remember all over again why you fell in love in the first place. Yes, times were different then. Sure that was long before the kids. Before the stresses which now plague you. But it was real. It was so, so very real. And it still is. Even though you seem to have forgotten it. It was all so, so very real. It's still just as real. And believe it or not, it's equally as strong. Memories, you see, are powerful tools within the domain of the inner Kingdom of Heaven. They exist for a very real reason. Memories can either seem like a blessing or a curse, depending upon the perspective through which we view them. However, memories, themselves, are simply moments of days long since passed. Today, I want to encourage you to begin to remember all of the good. And for now, today, neglect the difficult moments. Remember that what you affirm you will continue to manifest and there can be no escaping that. So, for now, I want you to remember only the good and neglect the bad. If you were to be completely honest with yourself, the truth of the matter is that you've had a few bad and unseemly moments of your own, so even when remembering the bad moments, try to show a little more grace and understanding to your spouse.

When I wrote my best-selling book *Creating with Your Thoughts* as a follow up to one of my most popular books *The Universe is at Your*

*Command*, there was such an overwhelming thought of creation resting deeply within my spirit. For me, those books served to illustrate a literal turning point within my life and my work. Although I had been well aware of the power of the universal Law of Attraction for year prior, it was while writing *Creating with Your Thoughts* that I began to recognize just how timely and just how needed the principles of attraction are today – especially in today's world. As I wrote the book, I felt within me a strong stirring – an unction of the Holy Ghost – to share with the world just how powerful our thought forms can be. To this day, all this time later, I still receive countless testimonies expressing how the principles contained within the book revolutionized and transformed lives. I thank the Holy Spirit for allowing me to share such powerful and transcendent truth with the world. I'm humbled to do what I do.

Within the book, I shared the spiritual principle associated with memory. Often times, when coaching or counseling individuals who have been abused or who have suffered intense trauma, I'm sometimes asked, "Jeremy, why can't I be delivered from these painful memories?" The answer is that memories exist for a very divine and heavenly reason. Memories serve as a reminder of just how far we've come. They remind us of moments of life experiences. Memories serve as the basis of our testimonies. However, memories also serve an even grander role. Memories can inspire us also. They can serve to remind us of how truly blessed we are and of just how much we truly have to be grateful for. Memories serve to reflect growth. Somewhere along the way, in the many stresses and difficult moments of your marriage, not only have you forgotten how far you've come but you've also stopped being grateful for it all. As a result, you've stopped seeing the journey as such an adventure. The marriage, now, seems like quite a struggle. Often times, when we think of a testimony, we think that testimonies are only relegated to the painful and the hurtful moments, reminding us of the pasts that we were delivered from. The opposite is also true, though. Memories serve also to remind us of the many good and the many joyous moments also. Just as our testimonies consist of the painful and seemingly disgraceful moments of the past, so, too, should they also include the many triumphs, the many milestones reached, and the many, many joys experienced. When I share my testimony, although I often think of the many growing pains of my own experiences, I also think of the many joys. Those joys are my testimony as well.

The scriptures make it quite plain the power of the testimony. We overcome and continue to overcome by sharing them. By reminding ourselves of them. Today, I want to encourage you to begin to remind yourself of just how far you've come within your marriage. I want you to remember the way it felt in the very beginning of it all, long before things seemed so very difficult. Long before you started to become so forgetful. Memories are miracles. Because we, by divine and intelligent design, are created with the ability to actually see our thoughts, we are given, also, the remarkable ability to relive certain moments. This is why, so often, when remembering certain moments, the feelings are just as real and just as intense as when the moment first happened. Memories serve as reminders; however they are also spiritual in that they operate as catalysts by which inner emotion and visualization are triggered. If you've followed my work and my teachings for any amount of time, then you know that I am an unashamedly strong advocate for the power of visualization. With each thought comes a mental, inner picture. And with each thought comes, also, a very real emotion. By meditating upon and focusing on the images of the past – all of those good and pleasant moments shared – you are actually reliving them all over again. You have the power to bring your memories to life all over again, through the technique of prophetic visualization.

It's not enough to simply see the images of the past as they flash before the mind's eye. We must also allow ourselves the feel the joy of it, as our emotions are intrinsically linked to our creative power. Creation is the correlation of what you see and what you feel, joined together and fueled with the force of intention and harnessed will and desire. So, as you begin to make a practice of looking back, I want to encourage you to allow yourself to feel the joy of the first kiss. Feel the emotion of the experiences as you look back upon them. When you think back to the wedding and to the courtship which preceded it, allow yourself to remember the love and the many wonderful emotions which flooded your life during that time, all that time ago. By choosing – consciously making the choice – to remember the good that was so very real and so evident in the beginning, I promise you, my friend, that you will begin to not only feel a sense of refreshing optimism but you will, also, begin to view your partner in a much different and more loving way. The love that existed within the beginning which drew into your life the love you had prayed for is the same love which must now be remembered if your marriage is ever going to be made whole again. The power lies within what you are choosing to visualize as you feel the emotion. This aspect of visualization is essential to the universal Law of Attraction and to the process of creating and manifesting what you want.

We need reminders sometimes. Reminders of just how truly blessed we are and reminders of what we've experienced in the past. These reminders – these spiritual images within – serve to not only encourage and to strengthen us within our marriages but they also play a vital role within the overall process of creation itself. As I've shared within my prior works, the moment we begin to visualize and take a front row seat to the images which flood our minds, we are being asked by the universe, "Do you want more of this feeling?" Although it may not seem so now, it actually is possible to rewire the circuitry of the human brain in order to feel more of the pleasurable and enjoyable feelings. Through neural plasticity, by focusing upon what we do want and upon what does feel good rather than upon what we do not want and what doesn't feel as good, new neural pathways within the brain are formed to solidify the feeling. Again, there is a very real spiritual correlation between feelings of emotion and the many diverse images of visualization. Visualization is a tool of the Kingdom of Heaven in that it allows us to literally view the emotions we want more of.

So, today, in closing this chapter, I want to encourage you to begin to make it a daily practice to take time to remember all the good that has come from the marriage. Take a moment to remember the many moments of joy and loving bliss. And as you do, remember that your spouse was there for it all. In fact, he or she contributed directly to those moments.

Those moments would not have been created were your spouse not present in them. Now, although it may be so difficult to remember, there is a very real reason why the attraction began in those very first moments of connection. There is a reason the love developed and grew to the point that you made the conscientious choice to exchange vows before GOD. My friend, although you may not believe it now and although it may seem quite difficult to remember, the reason was love.

# HOPE

*"Marriage is a choice. Your marriage can succeed if you want it to." – Jeremy Lopez*

Throughout this book, you and I have taken a journey together into the deepest and most transcendent elements of the Biblical law of Attraction, and it is my sincere hope and heartfelt prayer that the principles contained within this book can and will be used to not only restore a sense of wholeness to your marriage but that your marriage union will thrive as never before. My hope is that you and your spouse will rekindle the fire of hope once again. As I have said countless times before, there is always hope. The scriptures declare that hope maketh not ashamed and that there is a bright hope and an expected end for those who believe.

Throughout more than twenty years of success coaching and prophetic counseling, I have had the privilege and honor of connecting with individuals throughout the world who have come to me to inquire of the LORD in hopes of salvaging their marriages. Throughout every prophetic reading that I have ever given, regardless of the reason, there has always, always been a sense of optimistic hope as the Word of the Lord has been given. This is never more true than when couples come to inquire of the LORD concerning the restoration and the healing of their marriage. From the very beginning GOD ordained marriage to be a union of agreement and heavenly, spiritual partnership. Even from the very beginning, when boy first met girl within the garden paradise, love has existed and with it, hope.

Jeremiah 29:11 declares, *"For I know the thoughts that I think toward you, saith the Lord, thoughts of peace, and not of evil, to give you an expected end."* You're familiar with the words, I'm sure. So much so, perhaps, that they've become almost cliché to a certain extent. However, in order to begin to breathe new life into your marriage union once again, you're going to have to become more hopeful and more optimistic of its outcome. As I've shared throughout the pages of this book, based upon the divine, universal power of the Biblical Law of Attraction, what you envision, you will have. As I've said before, if you can see it, then you can surely have it. I want to ask you, my friend, when you envision the future of your marriage, what exactly do you see? Do you see even more of a continued struggle? More of a life spent battling a constant feeling of turmoil and agony? Or do you, rather, see a brighter future and an end result in which you and your spouse, together, continue to grow and to move from greater glory to greater glory as you depend more fully upon the voice of the Holy Spirit and upon each other? The way in which you choose to answer that question will determine your destiny, and only you can answer that question for yourself. Regardless of what your spouse desires and wishes to do, only you are responsible for the role you play. You are responsible for your own contribution to the union, and, as always, the universe is looking on in interest, careful to give you exactly what you want.

Faith is much more than a simple belief. It is much more so an overwhelming sense of hope. The writer of the book of Hebrews, in fact, states, *"Now faith is the substance of things hoped for, the evidence of things not seen."* *(Hebrews 11:1 KJV)* The evidence, though, is dependent entirely upon your own ability to see and to envision the end result of your marriage bond. As the old adage goes, the proof is in the mix. You, though, by the power of the Godhead which works within you, have all the necessary ingredients and qualities necessary to manifest within your life and within your home the marriage of your dreams. In his epistle to the church at Rome, the Apostle Paul wrote, *"Now the God of hope fill you with all joy and peace in believing, that ye may abound in hope, through the power of the Holy Ghost." (Romans 15:13 KJV)* Remarkably, in his epistle, the Apostle Paul alludes to the fact that it is not even enough to merely possess a sense of hope. The hope must begin to abound. It must abound so fully and so tremendously that hope begins to become like second nature to you. When conflicts arise, hope. When difficulties seem to arise within your marriage, hope. When your spouse is being so difficult that you feel driven toward a literal breaking point, hope. And when you begin to feel yourself losing hope, even then, continue to hope. Hope must become so ingrained within your feelings and your thoughts that it becomes a sort of reflex. Rather than succumbing to the despair which so often can accompany difficult moments, choose, instead, to hope. Hope is a very real spiritual muscle, but in order to work to its fullest potential it must be used continuously. It must be exercised, as all muscles must if they are to grow and become strengthened.

The truth of the matter is that it is virtually impossible to speak of the Biblical Law of Attraction without also speaking of hope. Hope, though, is much more than mere wishful thinking. Rather, it is a sense of knowing so complete and so real that it inspired action. Faith always requires action. All throughout the scriptures, with every account of transformational, creative power, we find that in order for the miraculous to become manifested, first, very real steps of faith were required. The miraculous never truly just happens, though it may seem that way to the natural eyes. Miracles, instead, require active and willful participation on the part of the recipient. Without a step of faith, the miraculous does not occur. From the account of the raising of the daughter of Jairus to the healing of the blind man, every miracle required active involvement. The miracle you seek within your marriage will be no different. Heaven is requiring active and willful participation on your part and, for you, the participation will require that you allow hopeful optimism to become second nature to you. By allowing yourself to view the good and to affirm only that which you do want, while choosing to not affirm the bad, you are placing yourself into direct alignment with the force of the Law of Attraction within the Kingdom.

When we are in alignment, miracles of transformation follow.

In moments of transition, I admit that it can be difficult to maintain this sense of hopeful optimism. Particularly when intense emotion is concerned. However, I also know that it is during those difficult moments that hope is needed most. The end result of your marriage will be directly tied to your very own vision of the expected outcome you hold within your mind. That is the power you, as a creative soul, truly do possess. I often find it rather remarkable just how very intrinsically tied we are to our own outcomes. As I look back upon my life and see the many, many successes I've been able to enjoy, I see that my very own mindset played a vital role. With grace and with faith must also come action. My friend, it's time to develop an action plan for your marriage, and the plan must include becoming more hopefully optimistic of the outcomes. By maintaining a sense of hope, in spite of the circumstances, you are literally signaling to the universe your intended desires. And through it all, hold fast to love. Not only is love worth finding, but love is worth keeping. In the words written long ago by the Apostle Paul, in his letter to the church at Corinth, *"And now these three remain: faith, hope and love. But the greatest of these is love." (1 Corinthians 13:13 NIV)* I wish you and your spouse success in all things, but above all I wish you love.

# ABOUT THE AUTHOR

Dr. Jeremy Lopez is Founder and President of Identity Network and Now Is Your Moment. Identity Network is one of the world's leading prophetic resource sites, offering books, teachings, and courses to a global audience. For more than thirty years, Dr. Lopez has been considered a pioneering voice within the field of the prophetic arts and his proven strategies for success coaching are now being implemented by various training institutes and faith groups throughout the world. Dr. Lopez is the author of more than thirty books, including his best-selling books *The Universe is at Your Command* and *Creating With Your Thoughts*. Throughout his career, he has spoken prophetically into the lives of heads of business as well as heads of state. He has ministered to Governor Bob Riley of the State of Alabama, Prime Minister Benjamin Netanyahu, and Shimon Peres. Dr. Lopez continues to be a highly-sought conference teacher and host, speaking on the topics of human potential, spirituality, and self-empowerment. Each year, Identity Network receives more than one millions requests from individuals throughout the world seeking his prophetic counsel and insight.

# ADDITIONAL WORKS

*Prophetic Transformation*
*The Universe is at Your Command: Vibrating the Creative Side of God*
*Creating With Your Thoughts*
*Crating Your Soul Map: Manifesting the Future you with a Vision Board*

*Creating Your Soul Map: A Visionary Workbook*

*Abandoned to Divine Destiny*

*The Law of Attraction: Universal Power of Spirit*

*And many, many more*

Made in the USA
Columbia, SC
17 January 2019